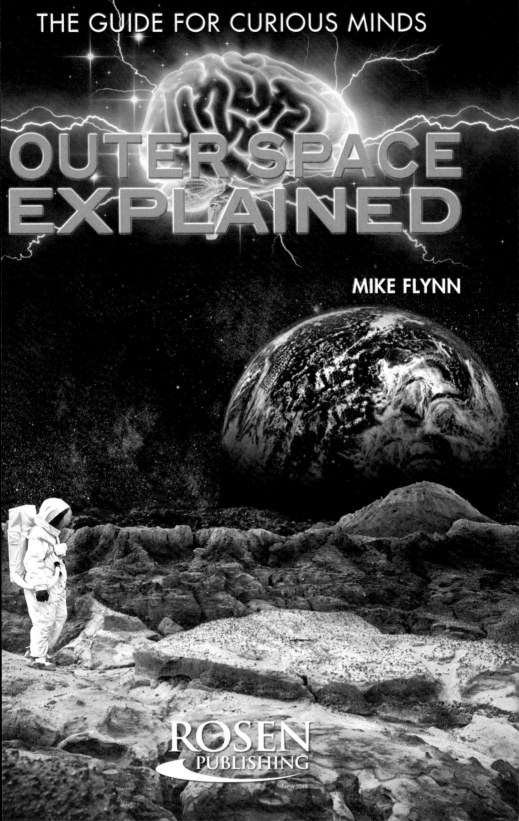

THE GUIDE FOR CURIOUS MINDS

OUTER SPACE
EXPLAINED

MIKE FLYNN

ROSEN
PUBLISHING
New York

This edition published in 2015 by:
The Rosen Publishing Group, Inc.
29 East 21st Street
New York, NY 10010

Additional end matter copyright © 2015 by The Rosen Publishing Group, Inc.

Library of Congress Cataloging-in-Publication Data

Flynn, Mike (Freelance writer)
Outer space explained/Mike Flynn. —First edition.
    pages cm.—(The guide for curious minds)
Includes bibliographical references and index.
Audience: 7–12.
ISBN 978-1-4777-8128-9 (library bound)
1. Outer space—Juvenile literature. I. Title.
QB500.22.F59 2015
520—dc23
                                    2014024372

Manufactured in the United States of America

© 2015 ELWIN STREET PRODUCTIONS www.elwinstreet.com

Contents

5 **ORIGINS**
The size of the Universe 6
A brief history of the Universe 8
Heliocentric Universe 11
The expanding Universe 11
Big bangs and steady states 12
Other universes 13
How it may end 14

15 **STUDYING SPACE**
Optical telescopes 16
Electromagnetic spectrum 17
Measuring distances in space 18
Worlds beyond – planets of other suns 22
SETI 24

25 **THE SOLAR SYSTEM**
A solar system 26
Birth of a solar system 28
Orbits 30
Types of orbiting bodies 32
What are stars made of? 35
What are planets made of? 35
What are moons made of? 36
The Sun 37
The Moon 42
The surface of the Moon 44
Eclipses 44
Comets 46
The planets of our Solar System 48
How much would I weigh on . . . ? 62

63 **STARS AND CONSTELLATIONS**
What is a star? 64
Life cycle of a star 66
Element factories 70

Distances to the stars 71
The constellations 72
Star magnitudes 78
Star companions 82
Nebulae 85
Death of a star 87
Going supernova 88

89 THE STUFF OF THE UNIVERSE
What is the Universe made of? 92
Antimatter 93
The forces of nature 94
The search for dark matter 98

99 LOOKING AT GALAXIES
What is a galaxy? 100
The Milky Way 101
Our intergalactic neighbors 105
Types of galaxies 109
When galaxies collide 112

115 SPACE EXPLORATION
How rockets work 116
Von Braun and the *V2* 118
Korolyov and the Soviets 119
Timeline of rocketry and space exploration 120
The space race 123
Vostok 124
Mercury 125
Project Gemini 127
The *Apollo* program 129
Space stations 133
The space shuttle 135
Satellites 136
Probes 138

Glossary 142
For More Information 144
For Further Reading 147
Index 149

ORIGINS

The size of the Universe

What do you see when you look up into the night sky? Do you marvel at the beauty of this fiery celestial ballet or simply wonder at the sheer scale of the heavens? Whatever thoughts or emotions cross your mind, there really is no getting away from the fact that the Universe is an awfully big place.

In truth, our brains are not really equipped to comprehend the sheer size of the Universe. Words like "enormous," "gigantic" or even "awesome" simply don't come close to conveying a true sense of scale, so let's start small and work our way up.

Imagine that our entire Solar System – basically the Sun, the planets and a few leftover bits and pieces – is laid out on the Center Court at Wimbledon in London, England, with Pluto at one end and the Sun at the other. Working at this truly tiny scale, how far away do you imagine the next nearest star would lie?

If you said Johannesburg, South Africa, you were probably reading ahead, but you'd also be right – and that's only our nearest neighbor. Even travelling at the speed of light, which would allow you to circle the Earth seven times in just one second, it would still take nearly four years to get there. That's a long way to go and also the reason why we tend to measure distances in space in terms of the speed of light.

Travelling through the vacuum of space, light moves at around 186,000 miles (300,000 km) per second, which seems very impressive. But even at this speed it would take 100,000 years to cross the Milky Way Galaxy, which is home to our Sun and all of the stars that you can see in the night sky. The journey to the next nearest galaxy would take an incredible 179,000 years, even at the speed of light. But what about the big one?

According to current estimates, cruising at the speed of light – which, let us remind ourselves, is an incredible 186,000 miles (300,000 km) per second – it would take something like 156 billion years to cross the known Universe.

Big, isn't it?

A brief history of the Universe

We know for certain that the Earth and the other planets in our Solar System orbit a raging inferno which we call the Sun. The Sun is a fairly ordinary star, one of about five hundred billion or so stars held in orbit in a loose spiral around what is almost certainly a truly massive black hole. Astronomers have named this spiral-shaped collection of planets, stars and assorted leftovers the Milky Way Galaxy.

Our Sun is tucked away in one of the arms of this spiral galaxy – the cosmic equivalent of living in Alaska. The spiral rotates at the rate of once every 230 million years or so, slow enough that these stars appear to be fixed in the night sky and can be used for navigational purposes. But it has taken us quite some time to reach this understanding of our place in the Universe.

The Greeks and Romans

The first recorded scientific theory on the nature of the Universe was put forward by the ancient Greeks, such as Thales and Anaximander. During the sixth century BCE they dropped the notion of a supernatural origin and proposed that the Universe had been created by natural means. The Pythagoreans agreed, creating a mathematical model of the Universe that was adopted by the Romans.

The Roman poet Lucretius, in *De Rerum Natura* (*On the Nature of Things*), wrote of an infinite Universe in which the interaction of things at the atomic level created a constant state of flux. This was a truly remarkable effort considering just how similar it is to modern thinking on the nature of the Universe.

The next major school of thought was led by Ptolemy. He described a finite Universe ruled by mathematics and God in which planets, the Sun and other stars were attached to concentric spheres centered on the Earth. He could not have been more wrong, but unfortunately his views were adopted by all-powerful medieval theologians.

ABOVE Frontispiece from Ptolemy's *Almagest* of 1496 that described the Ptolemic system of astronomy and geography.

ABOVE Frontispiece of Galileo's *Cosmic System* of 1663, featuring Aristotle, Ptolemy and Copernicus on the illustration shown here.

Heliocentric Universe

That was pretty much it until the sixteenth century when Nicolaus Copernicus revived the Greek idea that the Sun, and not the Earth, was at the center of the Universe. Copernicus' theory was supported by the systematic and highly accurate observations of astronomer Tycho Brahe (pronounced "Bra-hey") and adopted by Galileo Galilei. Galileo promoted this theory as his own, helping to spread it among European thinkers. He also came close to losing his life at the hands of the Church, who saw his ideas as heretical. Eventually he recanted but ended his days under house arrest.

Newton and the mechanists

Gradually, and inevitably, the truth became obvious and by the time Isaac Newton had provided a mathematical, mechanistic basis for our understanding of the Universe reason had finally triumphed over superstition. Newton's influence cannot be overestimated. Here was a man who, to his contemporaries, seemed to be able to read the mind of God, explaining His mysteries using mathematical proofs. Quite rightly, Newton's theories on the nature of the Universe remained dominant until the beginning of the twentieth century, when Albert Einstein introduced his theories on relativity.

The expanding Universe

Even before Einstein, however, some astronomers were beginning to notice that something was amiss. By the early twentieth century, improvements in the size and quality of telescopes allowed astronomers to see further into space than ever before and this improved resolution was turning up more than a few surprises.

The notion that the Universe was expanding had been around for a while. But in 1929 American astronomer Edwin Hubble was able to show that not only were all the galaxies in the Universe (including our own) moving at tremendous speeds, the ones that were furthest away from us were moving away the fastest. Suddenly the Universe was a very, very big place.

Big bangs and steady states

Having established a rough idea of the size of the Universe, astronomers began once again to turn their attention to perhaps the biggest question of all: how did we get here? First in line to answer this question was, not surprisingly, a man of God.

In 1931, Belgian priest and scientist Georges-Henri Lemaître proposed the theory that the expansion of the Universe was a consequence of the spontaneous disintegration (i.e., explosion) of what he called the "primal atom," a single entity containing all of the matter and energy in the Universe. In short, he claimed that it all began with a great big bang.

Although now the widely accepted view of the origin of the Universe, this theory did not find universal acceptance when first proposed. The English astronomer Fred Hoyle even mocked the theory and was clearly unwilling to believe that the Universe began with a "big bang." (Ironically, in using this term he managed to give the theory its popular name.) Hoyle, and others before him, believed that the Universe was in a steady state.

By this he meant that the Universe, although constantly expanding, had no beginning, will have no end, and when viewed from any point in time or space would maintain an average density because new matter was being created continuously to fill the growing spaces.

Unfortunately for Hoyle and his supporters, compelling evidence supporting the Big Bang theory appeared in 1965. Arno Penzias and Robert Wilson, a couple of radio astronomers from the

FACT
A millionth of a trillionth of a trillionth of a second after the Big Bang the temperature of the Universe was a whopping 180,000 billion billion billion° F (100,000 billion billion billion° C).

FACT
Hydrogen, which may soon replace gasoline as fuel, came into existence around 100 seconds after the Big Bang.

US, struck academic gold when they accidentally stumbled across microwave background radiation – essentially an echo of the original Big Bang explosion – while trying to eliminate radio interference.

The Steady State Theory was consigned to the garbage heap of history at just about the point when Penzias and Wilson picked up their Nobel Prize, an astonishing result for them considering that they thought the interference they'd detected was caused by pigeon droppings building up in their radio telescope.

Other universes

Of course, the above models are not the only theories on the origins and nature of the Universe. Leaving aside religious beliefs, there have been several intriguing ideas put forward in recent years. Among the most interesting is the philosophical idea of the Anthropomorphic Universe. Put simply, this theory states that the Universe is the way it is because the act of observing it makes it that way. In short, we define reality.

Another idea, and one that is increasingly gaining acceptance among mathematicians, particle physicists and astronomers is the notion of a Multi-dimensional Universe. There is certainly mathematical evidence to support the possibility that there are at least 11 dimensions (though some claim up to 26), the 4 that we can perceive – length, width, height and time – plus another 7 which are beyond our senses (and most people's comprehension). The universe measured along these additional dimensions is subatomic in size. As ever, only time and a few very fine minds will tell if either of these theories has any real validity.

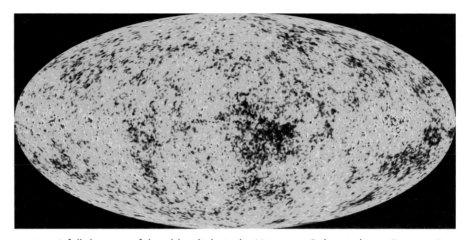

ABOVE A full-sky map of the oldest light in the Universe. Colors indicate "warmer" (red) and "cooler" (blue) spots.

How it may end

So, having examined how we may have got here, it remains only to decide on the final act. Will it all end with a bang or a whimper? The answer depends on just how much "stuff" there is in the Universe.

If there is enough matter then ultimately gravity will take hold and the current expansion will cease, giving way to a gradual contraction that will result in what has been dubbed the "Big Crunch." The fact that this may in turn trigger another big bang has been keeping philosophers, astronomers and sci-fi fans awake at night. It's an exciting idea, especially when one considers that we have no reason to believe that this will be the very first time that this has happened.

It is, however, thought more likely that there is not enough matter in the Universe for gravity to pull it all back together, and so the Universe will simply continue to expand indefinitely. Ultimately, all of the energy in existence will dissipate until the Universe will, effectively, be dead.

But don't worry. That's not going to happen anytime soon. By then our solar system and everything in it, from Shakespeare to *The Simpsons*, will be long gone.

STUDYING
SPACE

Optical telescopes

Despite being a truly remarkable organ, the human eye makes a poor telescope. Its small opening (the aperture) doesn't let in a great deal of light and the degree of magnification is fixed. The telescope was designed to overcome these two basic design limitations and allow us to look beyond the scope of our own eyes.

Optical telescopes – the type most people think of when they imagine a telescope – possess a much larger aperture than the human eye. This means that they can be used to collect much more of the light coming from distant objects, which greatly improves resolution and clarity.

Magnification is less of an issue with optical telescopes that are trained on the night sky. The Sun aside, even the nearest stars are so far away that no amount of magnification is really going to make them appear as anything other than points of light against the blackness of space.

How optical telescopes work

Optical telescopes can be divided into two different types: refracting and reflecting.

The refracting telescope

The refracting telescope was the earliest design and is usually formed using two lenses. The distance between the two lenses, which are commonly placed near either end of a tube, can be adjusted to vary the resolution and magnification required. Any light passing through the forward lenses is refracted (bent) before being focused on the eyepiece lens.

The reflecting telescope

The reflecting telescope produces an image with the aid of a large concave mirror. Light is collected by the mirror and focused on a smaller secondary mirror before passing through to the eyepiece lens. The reflecting telescope is also referred to as the Newtonian, after the English astronomer Isaac Newton who first used this design to build a telescope around 1670.

Electromagnetic spectrum

As can be seen from the illustration below, visible light represents just a tiny portion of the electromagnetic spectrum. Telescopes that can "see" across the whole range of the spectrum were developed so that we can gain insights into the workings of much more of the Universe than was previously possible.

10^{-6} nm			
10^{-5} nm			
10^{-4} nm		Gamma rays	
10^{-3} nm			
10^{-2} nm			
10^{-1} nm	1 Å		
1 nm		X-rays	
10 nm			
100 nm	UVIS EUV 55.8-118 nm UVIS FUV 110-190 nm	Ultraviolet	
10^{3} nm	1 µm	Visible light	
10 µm		Near infrared	
100 µm		Far infrared	
1000 µm	1 mm		
10 mm	1 cm		
10 cm		Microwave	
100 cm	1 m		UHF
10 m			VHF
100 m			HF
1000 m	1 km		MF
10 km			LF
100 km		Radio	
1 Mm			Audio
10 Mm			
100 Mm			

nm = nanometer; Å = angstrom; µm = micrometer; mm = millimeter;
cm = centimeter; m = meter; km = kilometer; Mm = Megameter

ABOVE Electromagnetic spectrum with highlighted narrow band of visible light.

LEFT Scale model of the Earl of Rosse's Leviathan Telescope, built in 1842, which was used to determine the nature of nebulae.

Non-optical telescopes

Non-optical telescopes allow observations to be made beyond the narrow band of visible light that we perceive. Astronomers use a range of telescopes which are tuned to different parts of the electromagnetic spectrum. These allow them to "look" directly at the Sun, "see" the natural radio signals from distant stars or, by using X-ray and gamma ray telescopes, construct images of distant black holes.

Astronomical telescopes

Astronomers use a range of telescopes when studying the Universe. Each is tuned to a particular part or parts of the electromagnetic spectrum and while many are Earth-based, the trend is toward placing ever more telescopes in space. These are usually to be found in orbit around the Earth.

Measuring distances in space

How do astronomers measure distances in space? They can't very well go out there with a very long tape measure to check lengths and widths and a pedometer is never going to suffice. Instead, they have come up with many clever and cunning ways of measuring these vast expanses.

One of the earliest methods of measuring distances in space effectively turns the Universe into a vast trigonometry problem.

Parallax shift

When seen from different points on the Earth's orbit around the Sun, nearby stars can appear to shift against the backdrop of the night sky. This apparent movement is called the parallax shift. By using simple trigonometry it is possible to calculate fairly accurately the distance to these relatively nearby stars.

Cepheid variables

Astronomers measure the distances to more distant stars by comparing a star's true brightness (or absolute magnitude) with its brightness as seen from Earth (its apparent magnitude). Cepheid stars are very bright objects that appear to pulsate. The time taken for the star to pulsate gives its true brightness. By measuring the difference between this and its apparent brightness it is possible to calculate the distance to that star. This is the most common method of determining distances to faraway galaxies.

The Hubble Space Telescope

Launched on April 25, 1990, the Hubble Space Telescope opened up the unseen Universe to human eyes, allowing us to view objects seven times more distant than previously possible using the most powerful telescopes here on Earth.

Essentially a giant reflecting telescope in orbit 600 miles (966 km) above our planet, Hubble sits well above the distorting effects of the atmosphere and offers resolutions 10 times sharper than those obtained with ground-based telescopes.

FACT
The distorting effects of our planet's atmosphere are such that even an ordinary hand-held telescope would be more effective when used in space than the most powerful optical telescope currently based here on Earth.

In addition to its 94-inch (2.4 m) primary mirror, Hubble is also fitted with cameras that are sensitive to visible light as well as infrared and ultraviolet radiation. Images are collected on these cameras using a charge-coupled device before they are transmitted down to Earth for analysis.

Communications antenna

Aft shroud

Aperture door

Solar panel

Forward shell

ABOVE The body of the Hubble Space Telescope.

The Universe through Hubble's eyes

The launch of the Hubble Space Telescope was a truly momentous occasion in the history of astronomy. For the first time ever we were able to see with our own eyes the true majesty of the Universe. From star birth in the Eagle Nebula to primitive early galaxies at the edge of creation, at a single stroke Hubble removed the shades from our eyes and changed our view of the Universe forever.

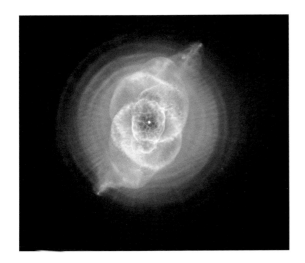

LEFT Hubble Space Telescope image of a dying star.

Why is it called the Hubble Space Telescope?

The Hubble Space Telescope is named after Edwin Hubble (1889-1953). He was a Missouri-born lawyer-turned-astronomer who is most famous for revealing something of the true scale of the Universe. His work on distant nebulae (vast interstellar clouds of gas) revealed that many of these apparent clouds are in fact galaxies lying at incredible distances from us. Hubble's observations established beyond doubt that these fuzzy "nebulae" were not part of our galaxy, as had been thought, but were galaxies themselves, outside the Milky Way. He is also noted for having devised a classification system for galaxies, grouping them according to their content, distance, shape, size and brightness.

FACT

The Hubble Space Telescope failed to impress on its first outing before it was realized that its reflecting mirror, the key component in the telescope, was misshaped. Astronauts had to fit the telescope with what is in effect a giant contact lens in order to correct the fault.

Worlds beyond – planets of other suns

Having established where we are and how long we've been here – if not yet why we are here – scientists inevitably turned their attention to perhaps the most important question ever to face the human race: are we alone?

It seems inconceivable to the human mind that, given the vast scale of the Universe, we should be the only intelligent inhabitants. But, to use the words of a well-known particle physicist and sceptic Enrico Fermi, where is everybody?

Back in the 1960s, the search began for Earth-like planets in orbit around distant stars. At the time, telescopes were not powerful enough to be able to pick out an Earth-sized planet anywhere outside of our Solar System – the light coming from the star it would

ABOVE A Hubble Space Telescope image showing galaxy Centaurus A, Earth's nearest active galaxy.

be orbiting would also make it all but invisible. This situation has barely improved since then. So, how do we find a distant planet if we have no chance of seeing it?

Star wobble

Everything with mass can exert a gravitational influence on anything else with mass. The Earth, for example, is kept in orbit by the gravitational pull of the Sun, which in turn experiences a corresponding tug from the Earth as the Earth moves along its orbit. Although ordinarily we cannot perceive this, it is possible to tell the degree to which the Sun is being influenced by the gravitational pull of the Earth by measuring the amount that the Sun wobbles on its axis.

Each orbit of the Earth produces a regular wobble which, even if our home planet could not be seen, would indicate to a distant observer that there is a planet here. This same technique can be applied across space to any observable star, and since 1995 has been turning up more than a few surprises.

The easiest planets to spot are the large (i.e., Jupiter-sized) bodies, which cause a pronounced and relatively easily detected wobble on their parent star. So far around 200 of these worlds have been detected. Improvements in this technique have more recently been producing evidence of Earth-sized worlds in orbit around distant stars. Alas, so far we have failed to detect any form of life on these or any other worlds.

FACT

In an attempt to communicate with potential alien civilisations, a radio signal was sent from the Arecibo telescope in Puerto Rico to a star cluster that lies 25,000 light years away. The earliest we are likely to receive a reply (if at all) will be in 50,000 years' time.

SETI

SETI – the Search for Extraterrestrial Intelligence – is the name adopted by a group of scientists who are dedicated to searching for evidence of intelligent life elsewhere in our galaxy. They use radio telescopes to collect signals from space which are then analyzed for potential signs of life. This might, for example, be a repeating pattern with no known natural cause.

With the exception of one signal detected back in the 1970s (and subsequently named the Wow! signal) there has so far been no evidence of intelligent life detected anywhere in the Universe other than on our planet, where its existence or otherwise is still a topic of much debate.

The Drake Equation

Frank Drake, a leading figure in the search for extraterrestrial intelligence, devised an equation (also known as the Green Bank equation) to determine the likelihood of discovering intelligent life elsewhere in our galaxy.

The equation reads:

$$N = R \times f_p \times n_e \times f_l \times f_i \times f_c \times L$$

At first sight this equations looks daunting but the equation breaks down as follows:

N is the number of intelligent civilisations that could contact us. It is equal to the number of stars in our galaxy (R) multiplied by those with planets that could sustain life (f_p), further multiplied by those that are Earth-like (n_e), the probability that life will begin on such a planet (f_l), the chance that this life will develop technology (f_i), and have the desire to communicate with us (f_c). The final figure, L, represents the average life expectancy of such a civilisation.

Using this equation, Drake predicted that there might be at least 40 such planets currently in our galaxy.

THE
SOLAR
SYSTEM

A solar system

A solar system is a self-contained unit consisting of at least one star which is orbited by one or more planets. There are, of course, variations on this model to be found in the Milky Way Galaxy but this definition covers the basics.

Our Solar System consists of the Sun (our star), eight planets, several dwarf planets, their various moons and assorted smaller objects. The Sun accounts for 99.86 percent of all the mass in the Solar System. We are only now discovering that our solar system may not be unique, although so far it remains the only place in the Universe that is home to life as we know it.

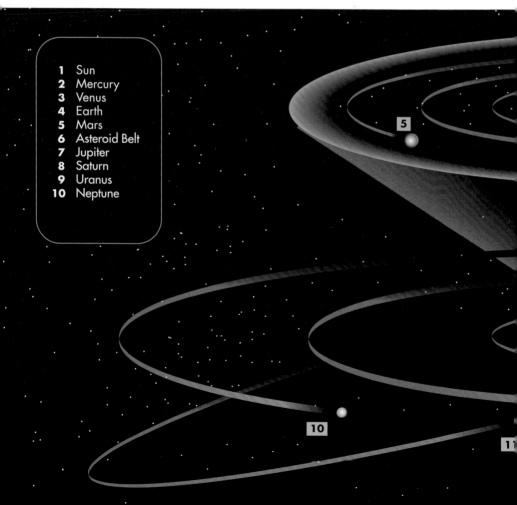

1	Sun
2	Mercury
3	Venus
4	Earth
5	Mars
6	Asteroid Belt
7	Jupiter
8	Saturn
9	Uranus
10	Neptune

For many years, people said that the Solar System had nine planets: Mercury, Venus, Earth, Mars, Jupiter, Saturn, Uranus, Neptune, and Pluto. In 2003, an astronomer discovered a large object out past Pluto, which he named Eris. This made scientists rethink the definition of "planet." In 2006, the International Astronomical Union announced that to be called a planet, an object needed to orbit a star and be big enough to both be round (gravity squashes large objects into spheres) and have cleared its orbit (the gravitational pull of a very big object pulls nearby objects into itself or sends them spinning off into space). There are many objects near Pluto, so it lost its planetary status. Instead it was placed in the newly created dwarf planet grouping.

Birth of a solar system

Our Solar System was born around five billion years ago in the fierce fires of a nuclear reaction. Over tens of millions of years a vast cloud of gas and dust had gradually built up, particle crashing against particle, clump against clump, each drawn by gravity to the center of a cloud. Over time the cloud started to spin, faster and faster, until the center began to bulge and our embryonic solar system took on the form of a spinning top.

All the while the central region, the core, was becoming increasingly dense, so dense that temperatures and pressures rose to a critical point and the core began to undergo nuclear reactions. Truly, a star was born.

The vast spinning disc of gas and dust surrounding the galaxy's latest star continued to rotate and over millions of years the same process that had given birth to our sun began to be repeated across space. Each of the inner planets, Mercury, Venus, Earth and Mars, began life as a few grains of dust, building up over time and combining with other dust particles to form clumps of matter. These clumps of matter inevitably attracted other clumps of matter and it was in this haphazard and random fashion that the planets were formed.

Beyond Mars (the fourth rock from the Sun) lies the Asteroid Belt, a collection of rocky and metallic objects ranging in size from a single dust particle up to the dwarf planet Ceres, which is 296 miles

FACT
The hottest surface temperature in the Solar System (other than the surface of the Sun) is to be found on Venus, which has an average temperature of 896° F (480° C). The coldest-recorded surface temperature in the Solar System is that of Neptune's moon Triton, which is a somewhat chilly -391° F (- 235° C).

JUPITER

Atmosphere

Liquid hydrogen

Liquid metallic hydrogen

Rocky core

ABOVE Cutaway of Jupiter showing layers of gas, liquid and a rocky core.

(476 km) wide. Some see the Asteroid Belt as a lost opportunity, a "wanna-be" planet that never had a hope of survival. Certainly, with the mighty Jupiter as a near neighbor there was little chance that the belt would ever yield a planet.

It's been claimed, and with some justification, that Jupiter is a failed sun. It was clearly a star in the making with a mass two and a half times that of all of the other planets in the Solar System combined. But there was insufficient matter in the Solar System to generate and support two stars and consequently Jupiter's light remained hidden.

As the first and largest of the planets known as the gas giants, Jupiter's rocky core is clothed in an inconceivably dense cloud of hydrogen and helium. Pressures at the center of the planet are such that the very core is believed to be sheathed in metallic hydrogen, an incredibly exotic material that can only exist at pressures we cannot hope to reproduce here on Earth.

Saturn, with its famous rings – which are thought to be the debris from a failed or destroyed moon – lies beyond Jupiter and was believed to be at the limit of our Solar System until the discovery of Uranus in 1781. Our horizons shifted further with the discovery of Neptune in 1846. Subsequent discoveries have expanded the known universe even farther.

Orbits

Strictly speaking, an orbit is a curved path, usually elliptical in shape and described by one object in motion around another under the influence of gravity. When we think of orbits we tend to imagine them on a grand scale – the Earth around the Sun, for example, or the Solar System around the core of the Milky Way Galaxy. But they also occur at the subatomic level, one example of which is the motion of an electron around the nucleus of an atom.

For many years it was taught that the Sun and the planets were in orbit around the Earth. This certainly seemed true to the casual observer but was a fundamentally flawed observation. First among modern thinkers to point this out was a fifteenth-century Polish scholar called Mikolaj Kopernik.

Better known by the Latinized version of his name, Nicolaus Copernicus proposed that the Earth rotated daily on its own axis and moved around the Sun in a year-long orbit. He published his ideas in a famous work called *De Revolutionibus Orbium Coelestium* (On the Revolutions of the Celestial Spheres), a ground-breaking publication that unfortunately contained a number of errors.

ABOVE Drawing of Copernicus' model of the Solar System from 1761.

FACT

Copernicus' *De Revolutionibus Orbium Coelestium* (On the Revolutions of the Celestial Spheres) was published in 1543, as he lay on his deathbed. It was banned by the Roman Catholic Church and remained so until 1835.

Among these was Copernicus' description of the circular orbits of celestial bodies. In short, the math simply didn't work. It took the intervention of a German-born astronomer, Johannes Kepler, to put things right.

Like Copernicus, Kepler was a strong advocate of the heliocentric (sun-centered) Universe but believed that the planets orbited the Sun in elliptical rather than circular orbits. In 1609 he published *Astronomia Nova* (The New Astronomy) in which he showed that the planets move in gentle ellipses around the Sun and that a (very long) line drawn between the Sun and an orbiting planet would sweep out equal areas of the ellipse in equal time. These two assertions are now known as Kepler's First and Second Laws.

Kepler's Third Law, published in 1619 in *Harmonices Mundi* (Harmony of the World), established that there is a distinct relationship between the distance of a planet from the Sun and the time taken for it to travel along its orbit. In essence this law states that a planet's journey along its elliptical path slows the further it travels away from the Sun, only to speed up again as it draws closer in its orbit.

ABOVE Kepler's model of the Universe, drawn up in 1619.

Types of orbiting bodies

Orbiting bodies range from the grand to the subatomic. For astronomers, the main examples are planets, moons, asteroids, comets and meteors.

Planets and dwarf planets

Within our Solar System, the largest bodies in orbit around the Sun are the planets. These range in size from the mighty Jupiter, which has a diameter of 88,734 miles (141,974 km) down to Mercury, which is only slightly bigger than the Earth's moon. Pluto and the other dwarf planets, such as Ceres, are even smaller.

Moons

Even Pluto has a moon. In fact, with the exceptions of Mercury and Venus, all of the planets have at least one moon. Saturn, in addition to

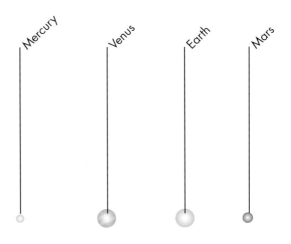

ABOVE A diagram showing the relative sizes of the planets, as well as Pluto, all of which are dwarfed by the Sun.

its magnificent rings, has 53 named moons and several more unnamed ones, many of which we just recently spotted for the first time. While the planets orbit the Sun, a moon orbits the parent planet. The best example of this is Jupiter, which, with its four principal moons – Io, Callisto, Europa and Ganymede – is essentially a solar system that has failed to fire up.

ABOVE Jupiter's four major moons, Ganymede, Callisto, Io and Europa.

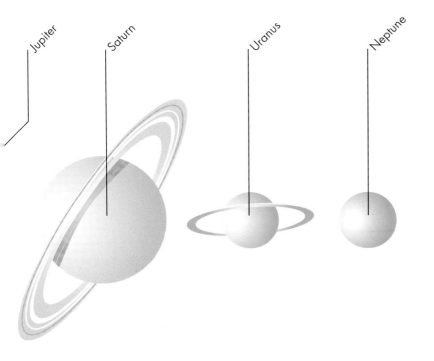

Asteroids

The next biggest bodies in orbit around the Sun are the asteroids. On the whole, these tend to be quite small. However, some are up to 620 miles (1,000 km) in diameter. Most asteroids can be located in a belt that lies between the orbits of Mars and Jupiter.

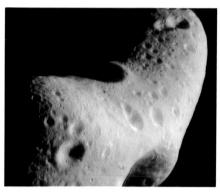

ABOVE The asteroid Eros.

Comets

Comets, which are little more than huge dirty snowballs, tend to come from the dark icy hell that lies beyond the orbit of Pluto. Occasionally the gravity of a passing star will knock one out of position and send it on a very long orbit around the Sun. On Earth we are from time to time blessed with the sight of a celestial snowball melting slightly as it passes near the Sun, leaving behind a characteristic cometary tail.

Meteors

Meteors really are the Solar System's leftovers. These lumps of stone and iron, drifting freely across space, graduate to the status of "meteorites" on contact with our atmosphere. Most burn up on entry, though a few small meteors regularly land on our planet's surface. The largest, however, have the capacity to destroy all life on Earth and have in the past been blamed for key events in our planet's history, including the extinction of the dinosaurs.

FACT

The Torino Scale rates the chances of an object – such as an asteroid, meteor or comet – colliding with Earth on a scale of 0 to 10, with 0 indicating no chance of a collision and 10 indicating no chance of humanity surviving such a collision.

What are stars made of?

A star, of which our Sun is a far from remarkable example, is in essence one huge nuclear reactor made of hydrogen and helium. Of course, when we on Earth think of these gases we imagine a barely tangible cloud of matter. Gas, as it occurs in stars, could not be more different.

The Sun is composed mostly of liquid hydrogen, which accounts for about 70 percent of its mass. The rest is helium, although traces of other, heavier elements can also be detected. Like all other stars, the Sun's energy and, therefore, most of the energy in our Solar System, comes from the thermonuclear fusion of hydrogen to form helium. This occurs at the core of the star and the resulting heat is then carried by convection to the surface. From there it is radiated out into space. This sounds like a straightforward process but it actually takes around one to two million years for the heat at the core of our Sun to reach the outer layers of its atmosphere.

Although we tend to think of stars as single entities, very many exist in combinations of two or even three, each caught by the others' gravitational influence and trapped in a dance to the death lasting millions or billions of years. Inevitably, stars eventually burn themselves out and, just like the stars of the entertainment world, those that burn brightest tend to burn fastest.

What are planets made of?

Planets are large bodies with dense rocky cores. They orbit a star or stars at regular intervals and on elliptical paths. The rocky core may be surrounded by a less dense mantle and a rocky crust (in the case of the Earth) or might have a thick, gaseous covering that is held in a liquid state under extreme pressure. The latter typically describes all of the gas giants – Jupiter, Saturn, Uranus and Neptune – in our Solar System.

Planets generally have atmospheres. These range from the near negligible in the case of Mercury through to the car-crushing dense greenhouse-gas atmosphere of Venus.

FACT
The Asteroid Belt has all the right ingredients for a planet but it would be a very small one. By comparison, our own Moon possesses more mass than the whole of the Asteroid Belt combined.

We call the time it takes for the Earth to orbit the Sun one year. But a year on the other planets in our solar system is longer or shorter depending on the planet's location. Mercury, which lies closest to the Sun, takes just 88 days to complete a single orbit while Neptune, the furthest planet from the Sun, takes nearly 165 of our years to travel just once around its orbit.

What are moons made of?

A moon is a relatively large body which orbits a planet in much the same way that a planet orbits a star, but on a far smaller scale. Our own Moon is a rocky sphere that we can see when it reflects sunlight down on us. Despite having a diameter about a quarter that of the Earth, like most moons it lacks sufficient mass to have built up more than a very thin atmosphere of its own – in essence the Moon is one giant piece of stone and lacks the surface gravity needed to hold onto many gas particles.

Ganymede is the largest of Jupiter's moons. If Ganymede orbited the Sun, rather than Jupiter, it would be classified as a planet. The Hubble Telescope detected ozone on its surface, so it is likely to have a thin oxygen atmosphere.

LEFT Ganymede.

The Sun

From its less than promising origins as a swirling cloud of gas and dust our Sun has grown into the medium-sized mature star that we know today. Formed as a truly ancient gas cloud collapsed under the influence of its own gravity, thus igniting the fusion process, the Sun has been blazing away for around five billion years and should be good for at least as long again.

The structure of the Sun

The core of the Sun has a diameter of approximately 280,000 miles (450,000 km) and a density roughly 160 times that of water. It is here that the thermonuclear fusion of hydrogen (to form helium) releases the energy that we have all come to rely on. As this occurs, 0.7 percent of the mass being fused is converted into energy, producing temperatures at the core in excess of 27 million° F (15 million° C).

Above the dense inner core is a region known as the radiative layer. Forming 70 percent of the radius of the Sun, this is the region where the heat from the core begins its one- to two-million-year journey upward to the star's atmosphere.

The radiative layer gives way to the convective layer. This is a 125,000-mile (200,000-km) thick region where heat from the core is carried upwards by streams of gas. As it travels through this layer the temperature drops from 3.6 million° F (2 million° C) to emerge on the surface of the star at a cooler 10,300° F (5,700° C).

FACT
The Sun burns up hydrogen at a rate of around 770 million tons (700 t) per second, yet 0.035 ounces (1 g) of hydrogen fusing to form helium produces as much energy as 600 million electric heaters might radiate in a single second.

FACT

At around 875,000 miles (1,400,000 km) in diameter, the Sun is 109 times wider than the Earth and could house over a million Earth-sized planets inside it.

The first layer of the Sun's atmosphere is called the photosphere. This is the bright surface of the star that we can see here on Earth. Perversely, having dropped, temperatures begin to pick up once again in this layer. They will eventually peak at temperatures of about 13,500° F (7,500° C).

Visible as a distinctive pinkish-colored layer during a total eclipse, the chromosphere lies above the photosphere and is home to temperatures of up to 36,000° F (20,000° C). Temperatures in the corona can climb as high as 3.6 million° F (2 million° C) before the light and heat that began their journey 2 million years earlier are cast out into space.

Solar flares

Angry, violent flashes of magnetic energy tear through the Sun's chromosphere flinging charged particles out into space. Usually lasting no more than 20 minutes or so, these cosmic tantrums are commonly called solar flares. The amount of energy released is the equivalent of millions of 1 million-ton (1-Mt) hydrogen bombs exploding at the same time.

Sunspots

Super strong magnetic fields on the surface of the Sun produce groups of dark patches known as sunspots. They seem dark because they are cooler than surrounding areas. Appearing mostly around the equator, sunspots can last for as long as six months.

Prominences

Breathtaking clouds of raging gas roar across the Sun's upper chromosphere forming arcs of fire known as prominences. Sometimes, if the fields become unstable, the prominences will erupt and rise off the Sun in just a few hours.

Solar cycle

Magnetic fields act to slow the flow of heat to the surface of the Sun, creating solar flares, sunspots and prominences in an 11-year tide known as the solar cycle.

BELOW The dark patches shown are the Sun's sunspots.

BELOW This spectacular image shows the Sun's fiery prominences.

FACT
When you look at the Sun you are effectively looking back in time as light from the Sun takes 8.3 minutes to reach us here on Earth.

Chromosphere

Convective zone

Corona

Photosphere

Radiative zone

Visible, IR and UV radiation

Radio emission

Neutrinos

Energetic particles

X radiation

Prominence

Coronal loops

Hydrogen-burning core

Bright spots and short-lived magnetic regions

ABOVE Key features of the Sun.

FACT
Everything that is critical to your survival, from the food that you eat to the fossil fuels that you burn, gets its energy from sunlight. Even wind power relies on energy from the Sun to heat the atmosphere and create wind currents.

Death of a star

The life-giving energy that we receive from the Sun is released when hydrogen atoms in the core of the star fuse together to form helium. This process has been going on for a very long time – around five billion years in fact – and should continue for another five billion years, after which most of the hydrogen at the Sun's core will have been used up.

Under the irresistible pressure of gravity, the core, no longer able to support itself, will begin to collapse as it begins the process of dying. Like a pressure cooker on the brink of blowing up, this slow contraction will push up pressures and temperatures at the heart of the star.

Any remaining hydrogen will fuse to form helium in a shell around the core, releasing enormous amounts of energy. This will cause the outer layers of the Sun to swell horribly as it takes on the form of a red giant. Soon our parent star, the supporter of all life on Earth, will consume both Mercury and Venus, stopping just short of the Earth. Then our fiery new neighbor will turn the surface of our planet into Hell's very own desert.

The core will become hot enough to cause the helium to fuse into carbon. When the helium fuel runs out, the core will expand and cool. The next stage is that the outer layers of our red giant sun will gradually drift off into space, forming what is referred to as a planetary nebula. The remaining core will then dim little by little, ending its days as a fading white dwarf star where once it shone a bright light on civilization.

The Moon

The origins of the Moon remain a mystery. The Earth's only natural satellite is an airless, lifeless, barren and dusty rock, its surface pitted by countless collisions with cosmic debris, and yet it remains the most arresting sight in the night sky.

ABOVE The Moon, showing its rocky surface.

The formation of the Moon

We can be fairly certain that the Earth and the Moon were formed at roughly the same time. Beyond that we can do little more than guess. The Moon may have formed alongside the Earth, making it a constant companion for the last four and half billion years or so. Alternatively, it may have become captured by the gravitational influence of the Earth at a later date, although this seems unlikely as the resulting heat would have melted both the Earth and the Moon.

The current most popular theory is that the Moon formed when the Earth was hit by a Mars-sized asteroid, a mighty collision that sent enough matter out into orbit around the Earth for the Moon to form from the resulting debris.

Phases of the Moon

For those who don't already know, the Moon orbits the Earth once every month. This ash-gray rock is visible on Earth whenever light from the Sun is reflected by its surface. Depending on the positions of the Earth and the Moon in relation to the Sun, the amount of the Moon's surface we can see in the night sky varies. These variations, during which the Moon seems to disappear before reappearing as a slim crescent that gradually grows to a full circle, are known as the phases of the Moon.

ABOVE The phases of the Moon.

The surface of the Moon

Pitted, scarred and dusty, the surface of the Moon has changed little in billions of years aside from suffering the obvious effects of meteorite and other impacts. Acting as a shield against certain death, the Moon has caught many an extinction-level meteorite or asteroid before it travelled that last quarter of a million miles or so and wiped out life as we know it. Up to 187 miles (300 km) across, the resulting craters can still be seen easily from Earth, highlighted against the surface of the Moon by huge, bright rays of ejecta which earn these battle scars the name "ray craters."

BELOW The crater Tycho, a ray crater on the near side of the Moon.

Eclipses

An eclipse is a natural occurrence, the result of the constant cosmic ballet performed by bodies in motion through space. A solar eclipse occurs when the Moon passes between us and the Sun, blocking the light from our parent star and casting a shadow over part of the surface of our planet. A lunar eclipse can be seen when the Earth passes between the full Moon and the Sun, casting a shadow over the surface of the Moon.

Solar eclipses occur once or twice a year and are only visible in the area of shadow cast by the Moon. This shadow is around 100 miles (160 km) wide. Lunar eclipses occur two or three times a year and can be seen from any point on the Earth facing the full Moon.

A total solar eclipse is probably a relatively rare event anywhere in the galaxy. We have the opportunity to see them here on Earth because our Sun, although 400 times wider than the Moon, is also 400 times further away from us than the Moon. This remarkable coincidence means that they both appear to be roughly the same size in the sky. This means that when the Moon passes in front of the Sun, for the observer on Earth it blocks out the light from the star.

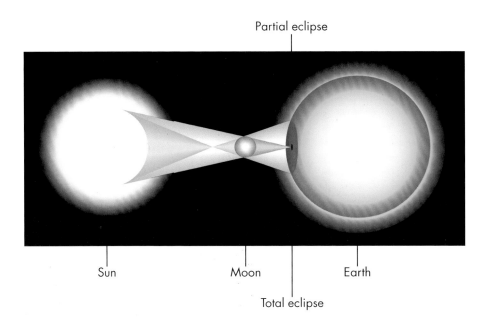

ABOVE The Moon casts a shadow on Earth during a solar eclipse.

Comets

Occasionally called "God's snowballs," comets originate in the coldest and darkest region of the Solar System. Hanging loose beyond the orbit of Pluto, these dirty snowballs, which are little more than lumps of rock and dust held together by ice and frozen gas, are occasionally knocked into an elliptical orbit around the Sun by the gravitational influence of a passing star. Depending on the path it follows the comet may become caught in a predictable orbit and be recognized as a regular visitor to our part of space. Alternatively, it may pass just once by the Sun and head off into space from which it is unlikely to return during our lifetime.

Comets produce no light of their own but instead reflect light from the Sun. As a comet gets closer to the Sun its crust begins to melt, producing a cloud of gas and dust which is known as the coma or "head" of the comet. A tail of gas is also released which, because it is deflected by the solar wind, always points away from the Sun. Although comets may be as large as 6.2 miles (10 km) in diameter, each pass around the Sun causes the comet to lose matter until eventually the giant snowball melts and disappears for ever.

In pre-scientific times, comets were often seen as harbingers of doom, a blazing message written large across the sky by the gods (or God). Sometimes, and purely by coincidence, the arrival of a comet did coincide with a significant event. This is hardly surprising given the frequency with which some of these comets return to our skies.

RIGHT The Borrelly Comet, showing its tail across the sky.

Major Comets	Discovered	Discoverer	Last (recorded) visit	Next visit	Period (years)
Halley	240 BCE	First sighted in antiquity	1986	2061	76
Kirch's	1680	Gottfried Kirch	1681	11036	9,355
Biela	1772	Wilhelm von Biela (1826)	1852	Broke up in 1852	Not available
Encke	1786	Johann Encke	2003	2007	3.28
Faye	1843	Hervé-Auguste-Etienne-Albans Faye	1999	2006	7.34
Swift-Tuttle, aka Kegler (responsible for the Perseids meteor shower)	1862	Ernst Wilhelm Leberecht Tempel and Lewis Swift	1992	2126	About 130
Wolf	1884	Max Wolf	2000	2009	8.21
Daylight Comet	1910	Multiple observers	1910	4144877	4,141,057
Arend-Roland	1957	Silvain Arend and Georges Roland	1957	Unknown	Unknown
Gehrels (78P)	1973	Tom Gehrels	1998/9	2012	5.5
Kohoutek	1973	Lubos Kohoutek	1973	76973	75,000
Howell (88P)	1981	Ellen Howell	1997	2009	7.2
Shoemaker-Levy 9	1993	Eugene and Carolyn Shoemaker and David Levy	1994	Impacted Jupiter	Not available
Hale-Bopp	1995	Alan Hale and Thomas Bopp	None	4377	2,380
Hyakutake	1996	Yuji Hyakutake	1996	31496	29,500
2001 Q4 (NEAT)	2001	NEAT comet search program	2004	Unknown	Unknown
2002 T7 (LINEAR)	2002	LINEAR comet search program	None	Unknown	Unknown

The planets of our Solar System

Mercury

The closest planet to the Sun is the smallest one in the Solar System. The scarred and cratered surface covers a huge iron core, which accounts for 80 percent of the planet's mass. The surface gravity of Mercury is too weak to hold a significant atmosphere in place, leading to an extremely broad range of temperatures during a single rotation.

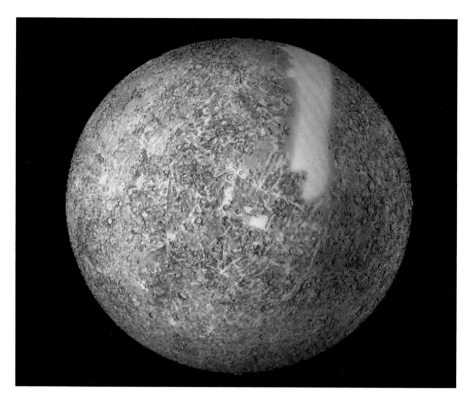

Average distance from Sun: *36.19 million miles (57.91 million km)*
Diameter at equator: *3,049 miles (4,879 km)*
Orbital period: *87.97 Earth days*
Surface temperature: *-299° F to 842° F (-184° C to 450° C)*

Venus

The second rock from the Sun is a giant greenhouse of a planet shrouded in dense yellow clouds containing sulfuric acid. With atmospheric pressures 90 times those on Earth and surface temperatures even higher than those on Mercury, Venus presents an extremely hostile environment. Once thought of as a potentially habitable sister planet to Earth, Venus was for many years the ultimate destination of choice for the Soviet space program.

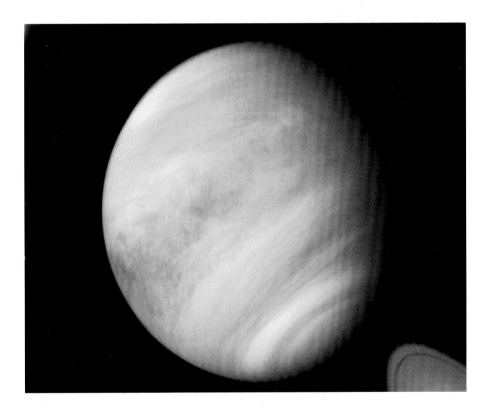

Average distance from Sun: *67.50 million miles (108 million km)*
Diameter at equator: *7,565 miles (12,104 km)*
Orbital period: *224.70 Earth days*
Surface temperature: *867° F (464° C)*

Earth

Home to the only life in the Universe that we know about, the Earth is the largest of the four inner rocky planets and the only one in the solar system to have an oxygen-rich atmosphere and liquid water. Life on the planet is protected from harsh solar radiation by a magnetosphere that is generated at the planet's core and which extends far out into space.

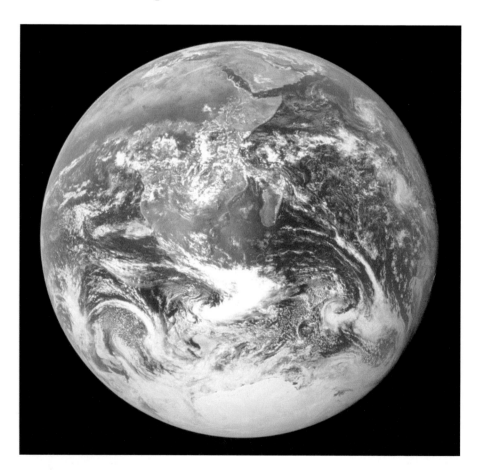

Average distance from Sun: *93.50 million miles (149.60 million km)*
Diameter at equator: *7,926 miles (12,756 km)*
Orbital period: *365.26 days*
Surface temperature: *-67°F to 158°F (-55°C to 70°C)*

The Moon

The daily tides on Earth are a result of the interaction of the gravitational forces between the Earth, the Moon and the Sun. Particularly high tides occur during a new moon or at full moon when the Sun and Moon are in line with the Earth. Low tides result from the Sun and Moon being at right angles to the Earth. About 239,000 miles (384,000 km) from Earth, the Moon completes its orbit every 27.32 days.

The Earth and the Moon are in synchronous rotation, which means that we always get the same view of the surface. The far side of the Moon remained a mystery until October 1959 when a Soviet spacecraft sent back pictures of the "dark side."

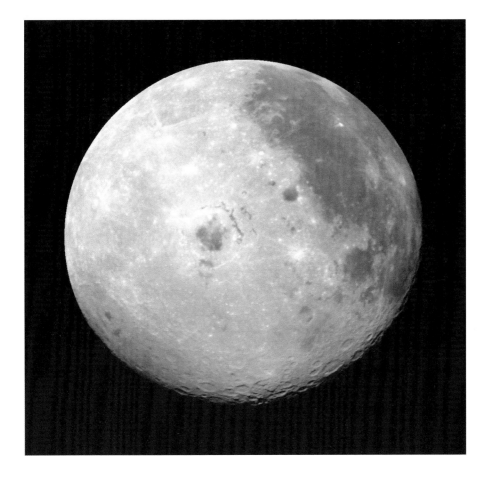

Mars

Famously known as the "Red Planet" on account of the reddish iron-oxide dust that covers its surface, Mars is the planet that most resembles our own. It has clouds, canyons, mountains, valleys and deserts and even white polar caps. Despite this Mars is a cold, dry and lifeless planet with a thin atmosphere that is composed mostly of carbon dioxide.

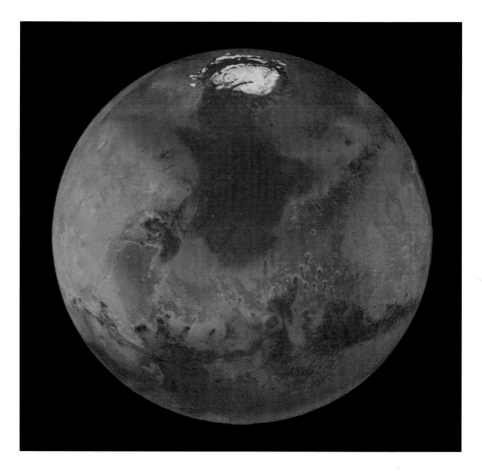

Average distance from Sun: *141.64 million miles (227.94 million km)*
Diameter at equator: *4,241 miles (6,786 km)*
Orbital period: *686.98 Earth days*
Surface temperature: *-184° F to 77° F (-120° C to 25° C)*

Jupiter

Mighty Jupiter is the king of the planets. A vast body composed mostly of hydrogen, it is in essence a failed star with its own mini-planetary system in orbit around it. The first of the four gas giants, Jupiter is 1,300 times bigger than the Earth and has a mass equal to two and a half times that of all the other planets combined.

Average distance from Sun: *486.43 million miles (778.29 million km)*
Diameter at equator: *88,846 miles (142,984 km)*
Orbital period: *11.86 Earth years*
Surface temperature: *-184° F (-150° C) (at cloud top)*

The moons of Jupiter

Jupiter has 50 named moons, the most important of which are known as the Galileans, named for Galileo Galilei, who discovered them when he looked at the heavens through his telescope in 1609. The German astronomer Simon Marius would later claim to have seen the moons first. He also named them. These moons are similar in size to the Earth's moon and offer some of the most interesting sights in the solar system.

Io – the first of the Galilean moons of Jupiter is fiery Io. Its proximity to Jupiter means that it is constantly being churned by the gravitational influence of this failed star. This drives volcanic activity in an otherwise frozen region of space and leaves it with a surface of vivid reds and oranges which are believed to be evidence of the presence of various sulfur compounds.

Europa – the scientific community is very excited about Europa. Although clearly hostile to humans, this ice-covered ocean moon may just be home to life. There is the hope that volcanic activity deep below the ice crust may have resulted in a liquid sea with the possibility that life-forms similar to those found around deep-ocean volcanic vents on Earth may also have evolved here.

ABOVE Io.

ABOVE Europa.

Ganymede – larger than either Mercury, Pluto or the Moon, Ganymede has a diameter of about 3,400 miles (5,268 km). The moon is composed of roughly equal amounts of rock and ice. It is scarred with many impact craters and, unusually, its surface features long parallel "trenches," that are hundreds of yards (m) deep and hundreds of miles (km) long.

Callisto – the outermost of the four Galilean moons is pitted with impact craters which shine out from an otherwise dark and fairly featureless surface. Despite its relatively large diameter of 3,000 miles (4,800 km), Callisto is only half as dense as the Moon. Callisto has the largest-known impact crater in the Solar System, Valhalla.

FACT
Powerful winds dominate the atmosphere of Jupiter with criss-crossing jet streams, lightning and huge hurricane-like storms, such as the Great Red Spot. This particular storm has been raging for over 300 years and is about twice as wide as the Earth's diameter.

ABOVE Ganymede.

ABOVE Callisto.

Saturn

Famous for its magnificent and distinctive rings that were thought to be unique until 1977, Saturn is the least dense planet in the Solar System. Its density that is less than that of water. It has 53 named moons, 9 recently discovered satellites and 7 main rings, 3 of which are visible from Earth through an ordinary telescope. The rings are composed of icy dust particles and ice-covered rocks that can be as small as a grain of sand or as large as a house.

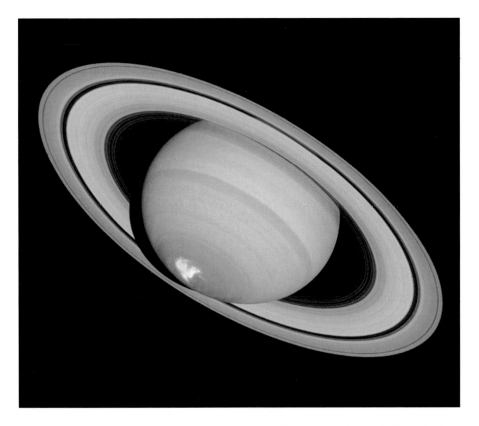

Average distance from Sun: *893.75 million miles (1.43 billion km)*
Diameter at equator: *74,898 miles (120,536 km)*
Orbital period: *29.46 Earth years*
Surface temperature: *-292° F (-180° C) (at cloud top)*

The moons of Saturn

Saturn has many moons but the first to be discovered was Titan, spotted by the Dutch scientist Christiaan Huygens in 1656. The second-largest moon in the Solar System (after Ganymede), Titan is also one of only a handful known to have atmospheres.

The bulk of this moon is made up of rock and ice but it is the atmosphere of Titan that has attracted the interest of Earth-based scientists. Rich in nitrogen and other chemicals, it was the relatively recent discovery of molecules of hydrogen cyanide in Titan's atmosphere that really got their attention.

Since hydrogen cyanide is one of the key organic chemicals associated with the development of life on Earth, some scientists have speculated that this moon may one day be home to some form of life. Titan's surface temperature of -292° F (-180° C) means, however, that in the unlikely event of life evolving there it would almost certainly not resemble life as we know it.

Most likely locations for life

The most likely locations for life in the Solar System, other than on Earth, are:

1. Mars: fossils of bacteria may exist all over the planet. Current life might be found deep below the surface, where liquid water may exist. Certainly, bacteria exist in similar conditions on Earth.

2. Europa (one of Jupiter's moons): may have liquid water beneath its icy crust, while strong tides and magnetic activity could generate heat. The combination could produce conditions similar to those near Earth's mid-ocean vents.

3. Titan (Saturn's largest moon): has a smog-like atmosphere rich in organic chemicals similar to Earth's early atmosphere; it also has frozen water and a hot core.

Uranus

An almost featureless planet lying in the icy depths of the outer Solar System, Uranus has a rocky core which is surrounded by a mantle of gases and ice. The planet's methane-rich atmosphere gives it a blue-green color which, aside from its severe axial tilt (97.77° to the orbital axial plane) and striking ring system, is the only distinctive feature of the planet.

Average distance from Sun: *1.79 billion miles (2.87 billion km)*
Diameter at equator: *31,763 miles (51,118 km)*
Orbital period: *84.01 Earth years*
Surface temperature: *-346° F (-210° C) (at cloud top)*

The moons of Uranus

Uranus is known to have 27 moons, all of which are made of a dark and dusty mixture of rock and ice. The four largest are Oberon, Titania, Umbriel and Ariel. These are relatively dull worlds displaying the usual impact crater damage one would associate with bodies of this nature. Miranda, the innermost of the major moons of Uranus, is an entirely different matter.

Smaller than the other major moons, Miranda was discovered in 1948 by American astronomer G.P. Kuiper. Its surface possesses a riot of interesting features, including enormous cliffs, wide open plains and deep canyons, some of which are up to 10 times deeper than the Grand Canyon here on Earth; these canyons appear on photographs as deep grooves in the surface of the moon.

Scientists have speculated on how these unlikely features may have formed without the usual forces of erosion. The most popular explanation is that Miranda may at some time in the past have been shattered by a collision with a large object only to reassemble itself later into its current rather haphazard form. It is perhaps as a result of these collisions that Miranda, which is thought to be made up of ice and rock in a roughly 50/50 ratio, is also home to a cliff face that is an incredible 3.5 miles (5 km) high.

As all the moons of Uranus are, Miranda is named after a character from a Shakespeare play, in this case the daughter of the magician Prospero in *The Tempest*.

FACT
Uranus was the first planet to be discovered in modern times as it is not visible with the naked eye. It was spotted by William Herschel, while systematically searching the sky with his telescope on March 13, 1781. It had been seen through telescopes before but was thought to be just another star.

Neptune

Similar in size and structure to its neighbor Uranus, Neptune is the last true planet in the Solar System. The atmosphere, which is bright blue in color due to the presence of methane, is actually made up mostly of hydrogen. Like the other gas giants Neptune has a ring system, which is divided into four distinct bands.

ABOVE Neptune (left) and its rings (right).

Average distance from Sun: *2.81 billion miles (4.49 billion km)*
Diameter at equator: *30,955 (49,528 km miles)*
Orbital period: *164.79 Earth years*
Surface temperature: *-364° F (-220° C) (at cloud top)*

FACT
The coldest place in the Solar System is Neptune's moon Triton where temperatures as low as -391° F (-235° C) have been recorded.

FACT
NASA's *New Horizons* spacecraft was launched aboard an *Atlas V* rocket in January 2006 and should reach Pluto in mid-2015. It will give us our first close-up look at Pluto and its moon, Charon, since no spacecraft has ever visited the dwarf planet and detailed images are beyond the scope of the Hubble Space Telescope.

The Kuiper Belt's Dwarf Planets

Out past Neptune lies the Kuiper Belt, a disc-shaped region of rocky, icy objects. Most of the frequently recurring comets originate from the Kuiper Belt. It is also home to dwarf planets, such as Haumea, Makemake and Pluto. Icy Pluto is a cold, distant world. It is so far from the Sun that our star would appear as little more than yet another bright light in the skies over Pluto. Its largest moon, Charon, is about half the size of Pluto and was only discovered in 1978.

The dwarf planet whose discovery led to Pluto's demotion from planetary status is Eris. Part of its atypical orbit of passes through the Kuiper Belt, while part extends far outside of it. Like all dwarf planets it is very cold. When its orbit takes it far from the Sun, Eris's thin atmosphere collapses and freezes to its surface, making it gleam.

ABOVE Pluto and its moon, Charon.

How much would I weigh on . . . ?

We have evolved here on Earth under the influence of gravity. The gravitational pull that the Earth exerts on us is largely determined by the mass of this planet. Your weight is a consequence of the interaction of gravity with mass. However, on another planet, one possessing a different mass, your weight would be different from that on Earth.

The following chart represents an interplanetary guide to weight loss (and gain) and is based on a starting weight, on Earth, of 141 pounds (64 kg).

Planet	Relative Mass (Earth = 1)	Resulting Weight
Mercury	0.06	53 pounds (24 kg)
Venus	0.82	126 pounds (57 kg)
Earth	1.0	141 pounds (64 kg)
The Moon	0.01	22 pounds (10 kg)
Mars	0.11	53 pounds (24 kg)
Jupiter	317.83	331 pounds (150 kg)
Saturn	95.16	128 pounds (58 kg)
Uranus	14.53	124 pounds (56 kg)
Neptune	17.14	157 pounds (71 kg)

FACT

One of the first people to find a practical use for Newton's newfangled gravity equations was Edmond Halley, who used them to show that the comets seen in 1531, 1607 and 1682 were in fact the same comet, which would be returning in 1758. It did, and is now called Halley's Comet.

STARS AND
CONSTELLATIONS

What is a star?

There is no such thing as a "standard" star. These enormous, hot, luminous balls of gas vary enormously depending on their mass, a factor which affects everything from the star's size, temperature and color through to its brightness and the length of its life. Even with apparently similar stars there are variations in their characteristics because of internal changes which occur during the lifetime of a star.

Most of the visible matter in the Universe is contained within stars, of which there are believed to be trillions in the Universe. (Our own Milky Way Galaxy contains billions.) The closest star to the Earth (aside, obviously, from the Sun) is Proxima Centauri, which lies a little over four light years away. The furthest stars from us can be seen in galaxies which are situated at the limit of our technology, glimpses of which can be captured by effectively looking billions of years back in time to the moment when the light from these stars began its journey to Earth.

In truth, it's highly likely that these stars are no longer there; what we see is a brief snapshot of cosmic history preserved as a consequence of the time it takes for the light from these stars to reach us.

The Sun is unusual insofar as it is a true lone star. Far more common are pairs of stars, multiple-star systems or clusters of stars consisting of several components including nebulae (which are clouds of gas and dust). These stars orbit a common center of gravity which usually lies at a point beyond the perimeter of any individual star. Often, in binary (double) star systems one of the stars will be too faint to be seen from Earth. In these cases astronomers may still be able to identify a binary system from the effects that the invisible star may have on its companion, affecting its motion and also impeding the light coming from the star by passing between it and the observer here on Earth.

RIGHT Star clusters in the Large Magellanic Cloud, taken by Hubble Space Telescope.

Life cycle of a star

It's been said that death is the only thing in life of which one can be certain, and this is true even for stars. They are born, grow to maturity, gradually fade away and then finally die. Death can come in many forms, some spectacular shows, others rather slow and sad, but it is certainly one of the things that we humans share with our cosmic companions.

Stars are born in huge clouds of gas and dust, the scale of which is almost beyond our comprehension. The Eagle Nebula is just such a huge cloud of gas and dust with tiny finger-like protrusions sticking out from the very top of one of its pillars of gas. The distance across a single one of these "fingertips" is equal to the distance from our Sun to Pluto, which is around 3.69 billion miles (5.91 billion km). Amazingly, any one of these fingertips could easily accommodate our entire solar system.

Star formation begins when the cloud of gas and dust is disturbed, an event which triggers an increase in density in a region of the cloud. Gravity causes the dense region to contract, pulling in more matter and making it ever more dense. At this point it becomes ball-shaped. From a starting point at just a few degrees above Absolute Zero (-460° F/-273.15° C), the cloud begins to heat up and then starts to glow. Now spinning at great speed, the protostar, or star in the making, begins to give out enough light and heat for it to be detected using an infrared telescope.

FACT
Stars cannot grow indefinitely and nature places a limit on the maximum size that a star can grow to. Anything more than 120 times larger than our Sun will be destroyed by its own radiation.

By now the original cloud of gas and dust has condensed at the core of the star and its temperature will be rising rapidly until the point, at around 18 million° F (10 million° C), when it bursts into life as hydrogen nuclei combine to form helium, releasing enormous amounts of energy in a process known as nuclear fusion. From this point on the life cycle of the star will largely be determined by its mass (the amount of matter it contains).

Low mass star

A low mass star, one with perhaps less than a tenth of the mass of our Sun, will by comparison give off a feeble glow yet burn for tens of billions of years. Called a red dwarf, it gets its name from the color of the light it produces, which indicates that its surface temperature is relatively low, usually around 6,300° F (3,500° C). Red dwarf stars are the most common type of star in the observable Universe.

ABOVE Red dwarf: artist's impression of gas giant planet orbiting the red dwarf star Gliese 876 in the autumn constellation Aquarius.

Medium mass star

A star of medium mass, which is to say somewhere between a red dwarf and perhaps half as big again as our own Sun, has a shorter but far more interesting life. This type of star is of particular interest to us on Earth as our own Sun falls into this category and its fate (and our own) is shared with other stars of similar mass.

Having moved from the protostar stage to the main sequence, which is the longest portion of any star's life, these stars will usually shine brightly for around 10 billion years. (Our Sun is around half-way through its main-sequence stage). Once most of the hydrogen fuel has been used up, the outer layers of the star initially begin to collapse inward until the effects of the corresponding rising pressure and heat cause the star to expand again and become a red giant.

While this occurs, elements such as carbon and helium begin to "burn" at the core of the star as the outer layers gradually drift off into space, creating what astronomers call a planetary nebula. Before long only the dense core remains, shrinking ever smaller and getting gradually dimmer until all that remains is a white dwarf, a cosmic ghost of the star that once was.

Large mass star

Stars with a mass at least half as large again as our Sun's live short but brilliant lives. They burn their fuel rapidly over millions rather than billions of years before expanding into red supergiants. When the core of a red supergiant collapses it does so with explosive consequences. This explosion, called a supernova, blasts off the outer layers of the star producing a dramatic flash that can be seen from millions of light years away. Should the core of the star survive the explosion it will cool and contract further to form a small and incredibly dense neutron star or a pulsar. A neutron star is composed either entirely or mostly from neutrons and gives off comparatively little light. A pulsar is a rotating neutron star which emits a strong and regular burst of radio waves as it rotates.

Super mass star

Stars with a mass in excess of 100 times that of our Sun are called supergiants. These magnificent creatures shine up to a million times brighter than our Sun yet pay a heavy price for their brilliance. After just a few million years all of their fuel is burned up and they collapse under their own immense gravity. When this process begins it will not stop and as the core grows still denser even light itself cannot escape. What was once among the brightest objects in the Universe now becomes that darkest, most intriguing and exotic of objects – a black hole.

ABOVE A black hole blowing bubbles.

FACT
Stars do not stay in the same position in the night sky –
they rise in the east and set in the west in the same way that
our Sun does. If you are looking at the stars through a
telescope you will see that they are constantly moving and
so would produce blurred star trails if left pointing in the
same direction for hours. For this reason astronomers
mount their telescopes on special supports that rotate at the
same speed and in the same direction as the stars overhead.

Element factories

Back in 1932 the German physicist Werner Heisenberg was awarded
the Nobel Prize for his work on Quantum Mechanics, putting
forward the theory that all elements could be built up from protons
and electrons, which is a roundabout way of saying that they could all
be made from hydrogen, the raw fuel of stars.

In 1938 another German physicist, named Hans Bethe, provided
a satisfactory explanation for how heavier elements could also be
built up this way. In short, he suggested that collapsing stars act as
element factories, with elements being built up from protons and
electrons at the core of the star.

Following on from this idea, the Indian-born astrophysicist
Subrahmanyan Chandrasekhar examined the final stages in the life of
truly massive stars. He suggested that as a star of this type explodes in
a violent supernova, the explosion will synthesize heavy elements
such as carbon, iron and even gold, blasting them across vast distances
in space. Over time, these elements will provide the raw matter for
everything in the Universe, from new stars and planets to plants and
living organisms.

As a carbon-based life-form, the elements from exploding stars
are part of your physical make-up. In essence, we were all once
simply stardust . . . and probably will be again.

Distances to the stars

The Universe, as we've established, is so big that words cannot really convey a sense of the scale of the thing. Distance measured in miles or kilometers means nothing beyond the boundaries of our solar system so instead we use nature's own yardstick: light. A light year is the distance a beam of light can travel across the vacuum of space in one year. Light travels about 186,000 miles (300,000 km) in one second, a remarkable 5.913 trillion miles (9.461 trillion km) in a single year.

Here is a three-dimensional view of the constellation of Orion. From Earth, the stars that make up the hunter of mythology appear as a coherent flat image in the night sky but they are in fact separated by vast distances. Each of the divisions in the illustration is equal to five hundred light years, the distance that light will travel in five hundred years.

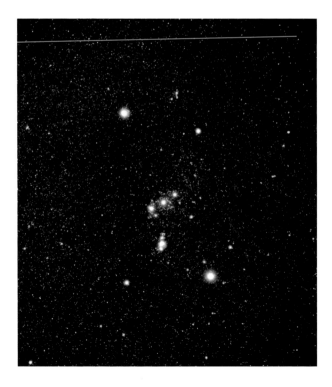

ABOVE A view of the constellation of Orion.

The constellations

The 88 modern constellations are given here with the hemisphere in which they are primarily visible (North or South). Constellations become higher or lower in the sky with the changing of the seasons. Thus many of them will be visible in different hemispheres at

	Constellation	Hemisphere most visible		Constellation	Hemisphere most visible
1	Andromeda	N	24	Columba (The Dove)	S
2	Antlia (The Air Pump)	S	25	Coma Berenices (Berenice's Hair)	N
3	Apus (Bird of Paradise)	S			
4	Aquarius (Water Carrier)	N/S	26	Corona Australis (Southern Crown)	S
5	Aquila (The Eagle)	N/S	27	Corona Borealis (Northern Crown)	N
6	Ara (The Altar)	S			
7	Aries (The Ram)	N/S	28	Corvus (The Crow)	N/S
8	Auriga (The Charioteer)	N	29	Crater (The Goblet)	N/S
9	Boötes (The Herdsman)	N	30	Crux (Southern Cross)	S
10	Caelum (The Chisel)	S	31	Cygnus (The Swan)	N
11	Camelopardalis (The Giraffe)	N	32	Delphinus (The Dolphin)	N/S
12	Cancer (The Crab)	N/S	33	Dorado (The Goldfish)	S
13	Canes Venatici (Hunting Dogs)	N	34	Draco (The Dragon)	N
			35	Equuleus (The Little Horse)	N/S
14	Canis Major (The Greater Dog)	N/S	36	Eridanus (The River)	N/S
15	Canis Minor (The Lesser Dog)	N/S	37	Fornax (The Furnace)	S
16	Capricornus (The Goat-Fish)	N/S	38	Gemini (The Twins)	N/S
17	Carina (The Keel)	S	39	Grus (The Crane)	S
18	Cassiopeia	N	40	Hercules	N
19	Centaurus (The Centaur)	N/S	41	Horologium (The Pendulum Clock)	S
20	Cepheus	N			
21	Cetus (The Whale)	N/S	42	Hydra (The Water Serpent)	N/S
22	Chamaeleon	S	43	Hydrus (The Lesser Water Snake)	S
23	Circinus (The Drafting Compass)	S	44	Indus (The Indian)	S
			45	Lacerta (The Lizard)	N

different times of the year, while some will be visible to both hemispheres for much of the time.

Where a star is visible in both hemispheres for significant parts of the year, it is marked N/S on this chart.

	Constellation	Hemisphere most visible		Constellation	Hemisphere most visible
46	Leo (The Lion)	N/S	70	Reticulum (The Reticle)	S
47	Leo Minor (The Lesser Lion)	N	71	Sagitta (The Arrow)	N
48	Lepus (The Hare)	S	72	Sagittarius (The Archer)	N/S
49	Libra (The Scales)	N/S	73	Scorpius (The Scorpion)	N/S
50	Lupus (The Wolf)	N/S	74	Sculptor (The Sculptor)	S
51	Lynx	N	75	Scutum (The Shield)	N/S
52	Lyra (The Lyre)	N	76	Serpens (The Serpent)	N/S
53	Mensa (The Table Mountain)	S	77	Sextans (The Sextant)	N/S
54	Microscopium (The Microscope)	S	78	Taurus (The Bull)	N/S
			79	Telescopium (The Telescope)	S
55	Monoceros (The Unicorn)	N/S	80	Triangulum (The Triangle)	N
56	Musca (The Fly)	S	81	Triangulum Australe (Southern Triangle)	S
57	Norma (The Level)	S			
58	Octans (The Octant)	S	82	Tucana (The Toucan)	S
59	Ophiuchus (Serpent Holder)	N/S	83	Ursa Major (The Greater Bear)	N
60	Orion (The Hunter)	N/S	84	Ursa Minor (The Lesser Bear)	N
61	Pavo (The Peacock)	S	85	Vela (The Sails)	S
62	Pegasus (The Winged Horse)	N	86	Virgo (The Virgin)	N/S
63	Perseus	N	87	Volans (The Flying Fish)	S
64	Phoenix (The Phoenix)	S	88	Vulpecula (The Fox)	N
65	Pictor (The Painter's Easel)	S			
66	Pisces (The Fish)	N/S			
67	Piscis Austrinus (The Southern Fish)	S			
68	Puppis (The Stern)	S			
69	Pyxis (The Compass)	S			

Star map

Here are the major constellations as they appear in the night sky. The constellations that you will be able to see will depend on your position on the planet. For the sake of convenience, we have divided the night sky into the northern and southern hemispheres. The positions of the constellations appear to change depending on the time of year with the result that some apparently drop below the horizon only to reappear later.

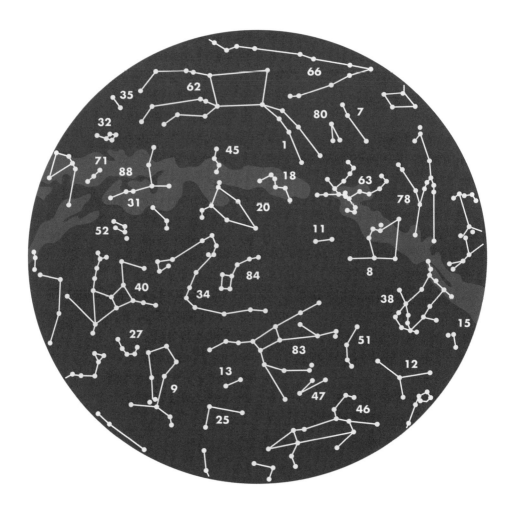

Finding a constellation in the night sky can be a tricky business so it is best to find a reference point that you can recognize – such as the North Star, when observing in the northern hemisphere – and then find your way from there.

BELOW Constellation maps of the northern and southern celestial spheres. Match the numbers to the numbers on the previous pages to see their names.

The zodiac

From our perspective here on Earth, the Sun appears to move against the background of the stars. The path that the Sun follows is known as the ecliptic, and a narrow band extending to about 9° either side of the ecliptic is called the zodiac.

In times past the zodiac was divided into 12 constellations, through which the Sun passed in the course of a single year. Originally intended as a way of measuring the passage of time, all manner of superstitions developed in association with these constellations, with astrology growing out of the belief that the positions of the stars and planets at the time of birth will influence the outcome of one's life.

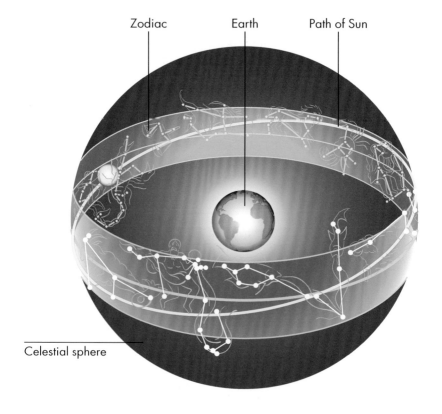

Zodiac   Earth   Path of Sun

Celestial sphere

ABOVE The 12 astrological constellations in a band around the Earth.

Most of the constellations owe their names to the ancient Greeks, who clearly had very vivid imaginations. Below is an example of an ancient constellation and the mythological figure imposed upon it.

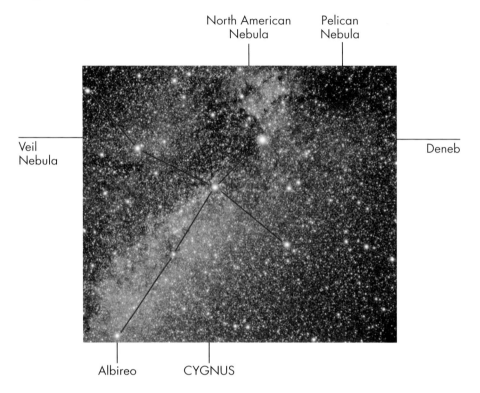

North American Nebula

Pelican Nebula

Veil Nebula

Deneb

Albireo

CYGNUS

ABOVE Cygnus, one of the richest constellations in the sky. Ancient astronomers believed it formed the shape of a swan with Albireo as the head and Deneb as the tail.

FACT
When astronomers pointed out recently that there are in fact 13 constellations in the zodiac – the 13th being Ophiuchus, the Serpent Bearer, which lies between Scorpio and Sagittarius – they were accused by astrologers of being "unscientific."

Star magnitudes

The brightness of a star, which is determined by the amount of radiation it emits, is measured in magnitudes. Confusingly, the brightest stars are given the lowest figures of magnitude. To make matters worse, there are two different kinds of magnitude: apparent and absolute.

Apparent magnitude is a measure of the brightness of a star as seen from Earth. Inevitably, this means that the stars nearest to us tend to appear brighter, while the light coming from those further away will spread out as it travels to us through space, making them appear less bright.

Absolute magnitude is a more realistic measure of a star's brightness. This figure is based on the magnitude of a star as observed from a standard distance of 32.6 light years away (10 parsecs). This removes the subjective element from the observation and is a far more accurate measure of the true nature of the star.

The Twenty Brightest Stars

Name	Apparent Magnitude	Absolute Magnitude	Name	Apparent Magnitude	Absolute Magnitude
Sirius	-1.43	1.4	Hadar	0.61	-5.42
Canopus	-0.72	-5.63	Altair	0.77	2.21
Rigil Kentaurus	-0.27	4.34	Aldebaran	0.85	-0.65
Arcturus	-0.04	-0.3	Acrux	0.86	-3.8
Vega	0.03	0.58	Antares	0.96	-5.38
Capella	0.08	-0.48	Spica	0.98	-3.55
Rigel	0.12	-6.75	Pollux	1.14	1.07
Procyon	0.38	2.66	Fomalhaut	1.16	1.73
Achernar	0.46	-2.76	Deneb	1.25	-8.73
Betelgeuse	0.50	-5.09	Mimosa	1.25	-3.92

FACT
Twinkling stars twinkle because of refraction caused by the movement of air in the Earth's atmosphere. In reality, the light coming from the star remains constant.

Starlight

Stars are categorized according to their spectral characteristics, i.e., according to the intensity of the radiation they emit. Starlight can be analyzed by passing it through a prism or, more likely these days, through a device called a diffraction grating.

This produces a spectrum of colors with dark lines which indicate the presence of atoms of certain elements in the star. This provides astronomers with what amounts to a list of ingredients for the star and is also very useful for determining the nature and probable life cycle of any given star.

Once analyzed, stars are categorized into one of seven main spectral classes, each of which has been given a letter of the alphabet: O, B, A, F, G, K, M. These seven classes are further divided into subclasses numbered 0 to 9. The Sun belongs to the spectral class G2.

FACT
Hipparchus, the ancient Greek astronomer who realized that the Earth is not flat, gave us our orders of magnitude when he described the 20 brightest stars he could see as being of the "first" magnitude while the least bright were said to be of the "sixth" magnitude.

Classifying stars

One can tell a great deal about a star from its color, but this can be deceptive. We often talk about something being "red hot" when what we really mean is "extremely hot." As ever, these words mean little when applied to the environment of outer space. The hottest stars are actually blue in color, with the coolest (e.g., those around 3,600° F/3,500° C to 9,000° F/5,000° C) being red.

This relationship between color and luminosity (brightness) can be plotted on a graph known as the Hertzsprung–Russell diagram. This is a simple device which plots a star's spectral type against its absolute magnitude. The hottest stars are plotted toward the left-hand

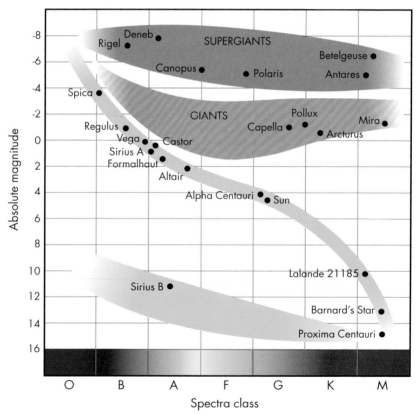

ABOVE The Hertzsprung-Russell diagram.

side of the diagram with the coolest to the right. Similarly, the brightest stars are plotted near the top of the diagram while the dimmest are placed near the bottom.

Once plotted, this relationship between color and temperature produces a broadly diagonal band across the middle of the diagram. Stars in this part of the graph are said to be main sequence stars, and this is where most stars are to be found for the majority of their lives. (Our Sun, for example, is classified according to the Hertzsprung-Russell diagram as a main sequence yellow dwarf.) The exceptions are the giants and supergiants, which are found above the main sequence, and the tiny dwarf stars, which exist below it.

Star mass

Stars can be classified according to their mass. This figure is an expression of the amount of matter something contains (density is a measure of mass per volume). When describing the mass of a star, we use our own Sun as a baseline. The Sun is considered to possess one solar mass. The dimmest dwarf stars may have a solar mass of only 0.08, while a supergiant may have a solar mass of 120. Most stars lie somewhere between 0.08 and 60 solar masses.

A star's mass (the amount of matter it contains) may be entirely unrelated to its volume (the amount of space it fills). Betelgeuse, for example, is a pulsating red–supergiant with an average diameter that is 650 times that of the Sun. This means that its volume is 40 million times greater than the Sun's volume. Despite this, Betelgeuse contains little more than 15 times the mass of the Sun, which means that even the air here on Earth is denser than the red supergiant Betelgeuse.

Type of star	Mass of a thimbleful	Equivalent on Earth
The Sun (main sequence yellow dwarf)	0.05 ounces (1.4 g)	Half a sugar cube
White dwarf	1.38 tons (1.25 t)	A hippopotamus
Neutron star	197 million tons (179 million t)	A fifth of the world's population

Star companions

Our star, the Sun, is unremarkable in many ways but one: it is a lone star. Around half of all recorded stars exist in tandem with a companion star in an arrangement known as a binary star system. Binary stars are locked into orbit around a common center by the force of gravity. The time it takes for them to orbit this point is known as the orbital period. So far orbital periods of between one day and a hundred years have been observed in binary star systems.

Eclipsing binary stars

The light coming from a distant star can appear to vary from one night to another. In many cases this is due to the presence of a smaller, unseen star in orbit around it. This type of arrangement is known as an eclipsing binary star system. As the smaller and dimmer star passes between the visible star and our observation point here on Earth, it causes a characteristic dip in the amount of light we can see. This periodic fluctuation in magnitude can be plotted on a graph. The resulting line is known as a light curve.

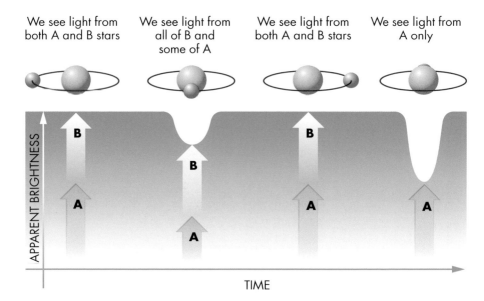

ABOVE The light perceived from a star with a smaller star in orbit around it.

Star clusters

Stars are often found in groups known as clusters. A star cluster is an arrangement of stars held together by mutual gravitation. These stars share a common history, having all been born from the same gigantic cloud of gas and dust. This means that they will be of a similar age and share the same chemical make-up. (They will differ from each other, however, because the real determinant of a star's character or type is its mass.) Star clusters divide roughly into two types: globular and open.

Globular clusters

Stars in a globular cluster will have formed when the Milky Way Galaxy was still little more than a spherical cloud of gas and dust. Globular clusters are found in or very near to the spherical halo which surrounds the center of the galaxy. So far about 150 globular clusters have been spotted in this region of the galaxy, most containing stars that are in excess of 10 billion years old.

ABOVE Globular cluster M31.

FACT
On the off-chance that there might be someone listening, scientists sent a radio message from Earth to the globular cluster known as M13 back in 1973. Conveying information about our Solar System, human beings and DNA, it will not actually reach M13 until some time in the year 30,000.

Open clusters

As the name suggests, an open cluster is a very loose arrangement of stars. The number of stars in any one cluster may vary from less than a hundred up to several thousand. Stars in open clusters are newer than those found in globular clusters and are situated in the rotating disc or arms of the Milky Way Galaxy. These are young and very bright stars which may be destined to drift away from the rest of the cluster under the influence of gravitational disturbances from other objects in the galaxy.

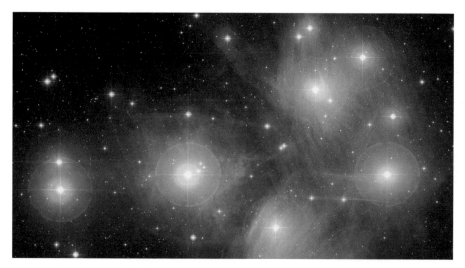

ABOVE The Pleiades (The Seven Sisters), a beautiful example of an open cluster.

Nebulae

A nebula is a cloud of gas and dust. Sometimes referred to as "star nurseries," these clouds constitute some of the largest objects in the Universe and can provide all the necessary matter for star formation. Nebulae are classified according to their relationship with light and can be divided into two main types: bright nebulae and dark nebulae.

Bright nebulae

Associated with star birth, bright nebulae consist of two main types: emission and reflection. Emission nebulae glow in the red part of the spectrum because they are heated by the young stars in their midst. Reflection nebulae, on the other hand, tend to appear blue in color because the dust they contain scatters the light coming from young stars in or around them.

There are two other types of bright nebulae, both of which occur as a result of the death of stars. First is the planetary nebula, which is created when a dying red giant throws off its gaseous outer layers to form an expanding shell of glowing gases. These nebulae, which are absolutely spectacular to look at, last for a few tens of thousands of years – a mere blink in cosmological time – before they disappear forever.

Secondly, a supernova remnant is a gas cloud that was born in the fierce explosion of a giant star. This casts enormous amounts of debris across space which is heated by the shock wave that results from the supernova explosion.

ABOVE The Trifid Nebula, an unusual example of a combined emission and reflection nebula.

ABOVE The Cygnus Loop (a supernova remnant).

Dark nebulae

Also known as absorption nebulae, dark nebulae are clouds of gas and dust which absorb the light passing through them and do not radiate any visible light – although they may radiate radio waves or infrared energy. If there is sufficient material in a dark nebula the process of star formation may begin and the nebula will undergo a change to become an emission nebula. Dark nebulae are sometimes difficult to detect and are best seen against a background of bright nebulae.

It should come as no surprise to discover that the Messier Catalog, the original (relatively) modern account of all of the visible features of the night sky, contains not a single example of a dark nebula. Invisible to the naked eye (and all optical telescopes other than by inference), dark nebulae are usually noted for what they are believed to obscure. In recent years the most famous of the dark nebulae, the Horsehead Nebula, has become an almost iconic image, embodying the beautiful mystery of space and the Universe and presenting one of the last truly unknown and yet familiar regions of the heavens.

Death of a star

As a star dies, which is to say when the nuclear reactions at its core begin to shut down, the star becomes unstable. In the case of a star such as the Sun this triggers a process that causes the star to evolve fairly rapidly into a red giant before it is transformed into a feeble white dwarf engulfed in an expanding shell of gases known as a planetary nebula.

Beautiful as planetary nebulae are, when a massive star dies things get a lot more exciting – and much more spectacular.

ABOVE The Helix Nebula, which is a planetary nebula.

Going supernova

A star must possess at least 10 solar masses to qualify as a supergiant. This means that it needs to have at least 10 times the mass of our own Sun. The life of a star that is this massive will end in an explosion of energy so powerful that it will, for a short time, outshine a galaxy of billions of stars.

Despite its size, a high mass star will use up its fuel over millions rather than billions of years. When it evolves into a supergiant the outer layers of the star will expand until its radius is roughly a thousand times that of our Sun. Inevitably, the star's gravity will cause its core to collapse. This happens at a tremendous speed – usually in less than a second – triggering a correspondingly galaxy-shaking explosion which throws debris right across space. The star can now truly be said to have gone supernova.

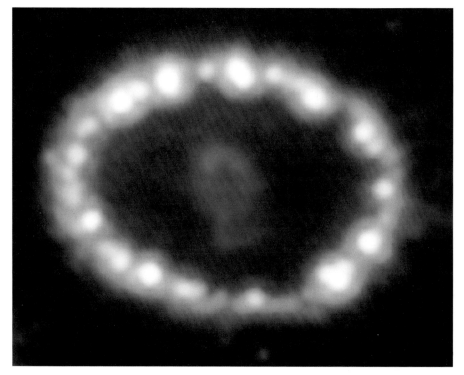

ABOVE Supernova 1987A, taken by Hubble Space Telescope.

Depending on the original mass of the supergiant, and the effects of the explosion, the remaining core of the star – if it still exists – will continue to evolve in one of two ways. It will either become a neutron star or a black hole.

Neutron stars and pulsars

If, after a supernova, the core of the star remains intact and enough matter remains for it to be between 1.4 and 3 solar masses then gravity will continue to do its job, compressing the star beyond the usual white-dwarf stage – which will be the fate of our Sun – and on into far more exotic territory.

Under extreme compression, the protons and electrons in the star's core will be crushed together to form neutrons. The process continues until the star, which you may recall was once a thousand times wider than our Sun, is little more than 20 km (12.5 miles) in diameter. The resulting object is called a neutron star.

A young neutron star spins rapidly on its axis and emits incredibly powerful beams of radiation that are channelled by the star's magnetic field into two powerful beams. Should one of these beams pass over the Earth it will be detected as a regular pulse of radio waves. Neutron stars that behave in this way are, quite logically, called pulsars. Pulsars can also give off other forms of electromagnetic radiation, such as intense X-rays and visible light.

The rate at which a neutron star pulses is determined by its rate of spin. A slow pulsar rotates perhaps once every four seconds; fast pulsars spin at a rate of about 30 times per second. Binary pulsars can spin at a rate of up to a thousand times a second.

FACT
In order for the Earth to become a black hole, it would have to be compressed until it had a diameter of just 0.4 inches (1 cm).

Black holes

If after a supernova there remains a core that is in excess of three solar masses then events tend to drift over into the realms of what might almost be called science fiction. With a remaining core of over three solar masses gravity is able to overcome any pressure from the matter at the core and, in theory at least, continue to compress it to the point where it has zero volume but infinite density. The remaining entity is called a singularity and it is at this stage that the conventional laws of physics appear to break down.

The intensity of the gravitational field thrown up by a singularity is so great that it creates a region of space around itself where nothing, not even light, can escape. This region is known as a black hole. The boundary of a black hole, the point of no return, is known as an event horizon.

Exoplanets

Exoplanets are planets that are orbiting stars outside our own Solar System. They are also sometimes called extrasolar planets. The first such planet, 51 Pegasi A, was discovered in 1995 by a Swiss team led by Michel Mayor and Didier Queloz. Since then, more than a thousand exoplanets have been detected.

While the discovery of each exoplanet is exciting, scientists are particularly interested in finding habitable exoplanets, or planets on which life could exist. This means they are on the lookout for rocky planets, not gas giants, and planets that are neither too close to nor too far from the stars they orbit. So far, astronomers have found several dozen planets that they think might prove habitable.

FACT
If a bag of sugar, which ordinarily weighs 2.2 pounds (1 kg) here on Earth, were to be taken to the edge of a black hole, its weight would increase under the influence of such extreme gravity to a trillion tons (t).

THE
STUFF
OF THE
UNIVERSE

What is the Universe made of?

The Universe, which is to say everything that exists, is largely composed of matter surrounded by not very much at all. That said, the "not very much at all" may yet turn out to include something rather important, so for now we call some of it dark matter.

Most of the matter that we can see is arranged in enormous superclusters of galaxies. Each of these galaxies is made up of billions of stars, some of which have planets in orbit around them. At least one of these planets is home to living creatures.

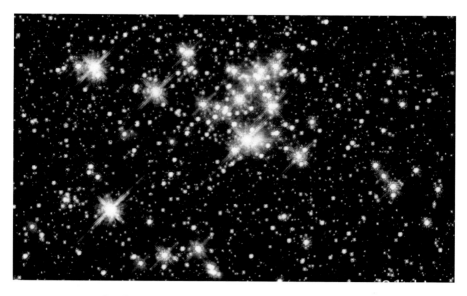

ABOVE A quintuplet cluster near the center of the galaxy.

It is believed that all of the matter in the Universe came into being during the Big Bang. Currently the only credible model of the origin for the Universe, the Big Bang occurred around 14 billion years ago when the Universe spontaneously exploded into existence.

During the period immediately after the explosion all that existed was radiation and an assortment of subatomic particles. As the Universe expanded, some of this matter condensed to form the stars, which are concentrated in the galaxies which, as we already know, are themselves grouped into superclusters.

All of the matter contained in the Universe is composed of tiny particles, which are invisible to the naked eye. Protons, neutrons and electrons are examples of these particles and they are usually found grouped together in the form of atoms – an atom is just about the smallest thing an element can be broken down into and still retain its basic properties. Even these particles, however, are made of smaller particles called quarks, which can be one of six types or "flavors:" up; down; top; bottom; strange; and charm.

Antimatter

As the name suggests, antimatter might be considered to be the opposite of matter. Certainly, most of the attributes one would normally associate with elementary particles – such as electrical charge and spin – are reversed in particles of antimatter.

Particles of antimatter are known as positrons and they cannot exist in close proximity to particles of matter; the particles annihilate each other, releasing huge amounts of energy in accordance with Einstein's theory of special relativity.

Some astronomers have suggested that antimatter galaxies may exist in the far reaches of the Universe, although others argue that taking such a stand is the scientific equivalent of writing "Here be dragons" on an incomplete map. We did, however, have positive proof of the existence of antimatter particles here on Earth when scientists at the CERN particle physics laboratory in Switzerland created nine atoms of antihydrogen. The particles existed for just 40 nanoseconds.

FACT
The Universe is filled with cosmic background radiation, which is an echo of the Big Bang explosion. This can still be heard as white noise when you tune your radio between different stations.

The forces of nature

The behavior of all matter in the Universe is governed by the four fundamental forces. These forces, or interactions as they are sometimes called, are gravity, the electromagnetic force, the strong nuclear force and a force known as the weak interaction.

The fundamental forces are currently believed to be transmitted via tiny particles called gauge bosons. Each of the forces has its own gauge boson and these are called gravitons (for gravity), photons (for the electromagnetic force), gluons (for the strong nuclear force) and W, Z particles (for the weak nuclear force).

The Grand Unified Theory

Since the early twentieth century scientists have been attempting to find a theory that will link the four fundamental forces and perhaps prove that they are all aspects of a single, primary force. The quest for this Holy Grail of science is called the search for the Grand Unified Theory. Despite the best efforts of some of the science community's finest minds – Albert Einstein included – this theory has yet to be proved.

ABOVE Albert Einstein in 1935 lecturing to the American Association for the Advancement of Science on the theory that the universe might be infinite.

Gravity

Of the four fundamental forces, gravity is the one with which most people are familiar. It binds galaxies together and causes apples to fall on the heads of geniuses and ignoramuses alike. Gravity is essentially a consequence of mass. Any object possessing mass can exert a gravitational influence on any other object possessing mass. The larger the masses of the two objects, and the closer they are to each other, the greater the gravitational attraction between them will be.

Gravitons, which are believed to be the carrier particles for this force, have yet to be discovered. An alternative but not opposing view, which is expressed in Einstein's General Theory of Relativity, states that gravity is a consequence of the distortion of the fabric of space-time by objects possessing mass.

FACT
Gravity appears to be the weakest of the fundamental forces. Some mathematicians believe that this may be because it is a force that is felt across 11-dimensional space and as such is spread a bit thin in the four-dimensional version of the Universe that we can perceive.

The electromagnetic force

All particles that have an electric charge, such as the electron, are under the influence of the electromagnetic force. This force acts between the atoms and molecules of solid objects and gives them their rigidity. It also holds together the atoms in water molecules and, should these freeze, it holds the water molecules together to form ice.

Magnets also behave the way they do because of the electromagnetic force. The carrier particle for the electromagnetic force is the photon. These particles are the same ones from which visible light is "made."

FACT
The Irish writer James Joyce was the first person to use the word "quark," in his novel *Finnegans Wake*.

The strong nuclear force

The strong nuclear force is at work in the nucleus of an atom, holding together the neutrons and protons. Protons have a positive charge and are constantly trying to repel each other – they would fly apart were it not for the presence of this force. In essence, the strong nuclear force is the glue that binds the nucleus of an atom together. Rearrangement of the particles that are held together by the strong nuclear force releases vast amounts of energy and it is in this way, through the rearrangement of hydrogen atoms into helium atoms, that the Sun and all other stars derive their energy.

The weak interaction

The weak interaction is probably the least interesting of all the fundamental forces. It doesn't bind galaxies together, it doesn't shine a light on anything or govern nuclear reactions in the core of a star, but it does glow in the dark.

It enables radioactive beta decay, which results in the break-up of the nucleus of an atom. By their very nature, radioactive atoms are unstable – their nuclei are home to too many neutrons. By virtue of the weak interaction, a neutron can change into a proton and in the process give off an electron (which in this instance is called a beta particle). What relevance does this have to your daily life? Well, it's the reason why your watch face glows in the dark.

RIGHT The rising Sun makes a dramatic backdrop for the space shuttle *Discovery's* rollout in 1997.

The search for dark matter

Astronomers have a very good idea of just how much mass there should be in the Universe. Unfortunately, the Universe doesn't seem to agree with them. In truth, based on the astronomers' calculations, over 90 percent of the Universe appears to be missing – the astronomers are certain that the matter is out there, they just can't seem to lay their hands on it at the moment.

Back in the 1930s, when astronomers were measuring the speed of rotating galaxies, they were shocked to discover that most were spinning at more than twice the speed they'd expected. So fast, in fact, that they should have been flying apart. But they weren't. Could it be that some kind of invisible mass, some "dark matter," was holding them together?

This dark matter, which is thought to be made of particles so small that they could pass easily through the human body without being detected, is now believed to be bound up in vast clouds of hot gas which surround clusters of galaxies in deep space.

Obviously, although this gas can be seen, the dark matter it masks cannot. But the fact that these gas clouds are caught in the gravitational influence of the galaxy clusters indicates that there must be a great deal more mass present than appears to be the case. If not, the gas would simply drift off into space. The latest calculations indicate that there must be at least four times as much invisible mass – or dark matter – in the clouds as there is visible matter.

At present astronomers are attempting to detect dark matter particles by setting up incredibly sensitive equipment at the bottom of deep mineshafts, well away from the distorting effects of cosmic radiation. Should dark matter ever be found it will provide conclusive proof of Einstein's general theory of relativity.

LOOKING AT
GALAXIES

What is a galaxy?

A galaxy is essentially an immense collection of stars which are held together by gravity. In among the stars one will also find lots of billowing gas clouds and dust as well as assorted planets, moons, asteroids, meteors, comets and perhaps even the occasional black hole. Galaxies range in size from just a few hundred light years across to enormous celestial beasts spanning over three million light years of space and stuffed with more than a trillion different stars. Scientists estimate that there are about 100 billion galaxies in the Universe. Rather than being spread out evenly, however, they tend to be grouped into superclusters.

Our knowledge of galaxies remains incomplete as it was only relatively recently that they were recognized for what they are. Using greatly improved telescopes that were invented and produced during the early twentieth century, astronomers came to realize that what had once been thought of as fairly nearby nebulae were in fact far distant galaxies. This led to some previously catalogued deep-space objects being reclassified, with the Andromeda Nebula, for example, being renamed the Andromeda Galaxy.

Back in the eighteenth century the French astronomer Charles Messier created a system of classification that still has an influence on astronomy today; it is the reason why many galaxies still appear with the prefix "M" (for Messier). A later listing, also in use now, was the New General Catalogue. This added the prefix NGC to all known galaxies.

In 1926, the American astronomer Edwin Hubble, who did so much to improve our understanding of the sheer scale of the Universe, categorized all the known galaxies according to shape. This approach imposed four basic models: irregular, elliptical, spiral and barred spiral. Later, in the early 1960s, a new and more distant type of galaxy was discovered. Situated billions of light years from Earth, the quasar remains something of a mystery.

The Milky Way

Our Solar System is to be found in one arm of a spiral galaxy called the Milky Way. The nucleus of the galaxy is about 12,000 light years in diameter, but the disc in which it sits is eight times wider at 100,000 light years in diameter. This disc is 1,000 light years thick.

The Sun shares this galaxy with around 500 billion other stars, many of which are concentrated in a dense spherical nucleus near the center of the spiral. The galactic center is believed to be home to a fearsomely massive black hole called Sagittarius A*. The rest of the stars in the galaxy are scattered throughout the four main arms of the spiral, which are named Sagittarius, Norma, Centaurus and Perseus. The Sun, which is about 30,000 light years from the center of the galaxy, is part of the Orion arm, one of several minor arms in the Milky Way Galaxy.

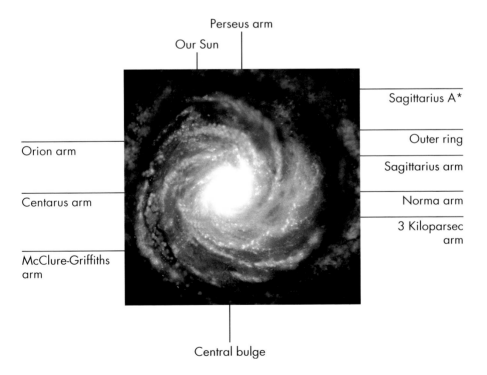

Perseus arm

Our Sun

Sagittarius A*

Outer ring

Orion arm

Sagittarius arm

Centarus arm

Norma arm

3 Kiloparsec arm

McClure-Griffiths arm

Central bulge

ABOVE Milky Way Galaxy, viewed from above.

BELOW Milky Way Galaxy.

The Sun orbits the center of the Milky Way Galaxy at a speed of around 138 miles (220 km) per second but even at this speed it takes approximately 250 million years to complete a single orbit. It is thought that the Sun has orbited the center of the galaxy somewhere between 15 and 23 times so far.

Radio continuum (408 MHz)

Atomic hydrogen

Radio continuum (2.5 GHz)

Molecular hydrogen

Infrared

Mid-infrared

New-infrared

Optical

X-ray

Gamma ray

ABOVE Milky Way Galaxy multiwave.

Our intergalactic neighbors

Our galaxy, enormous as it is, is only one of several in a relatively small cluster of several dozen galaxies that make up the Local Group. The Local Group occupies a region of space that is about three million light years across. Although this cluster has no real center, the two most massive galaxies, ours and the Andromeda Galaxy, form the centers of two subgroups.

The Large and Small Magellanic Clouds are the nearest galaxies to our own. The Large Magellanic Cloud is 179,000 light years away while the Small Magellanic Cloud lies 210,000 light years away. The use of the word "cloud" in their names is a throwback to the days when these galaxies were believed simply to be clouds of gas and dust drifting in space, a misconception that continued until improvements in telescope design revealed the truth.

After Andromeda and the Milky Way, the Large Magellanic Cloud and the magnificent spiral galaxy M33 are the next largest in size. The remaining galaxies are relatively small by comparison and are largely faint elliptical or irregular-shaped galaxies.

The Local Group is part of an even larger body called the Local Supercluster. This contains several hundred galaxy clusters and is arranged in a shape that can only be likened to that of a loose handful of string. The supercluster strings constitute the boundaries to voids that are truly incomprehensible in size. These voids separate superclusters from each other.

FACT
Though artists have made drawings of the Milky Way Galaxy, there are no photos of the galaxy as a whole. No man-made object, let alone a camera, has ever travelled far enough out into the reaches of space to be able to take such a shot.

The Andromeda Galaxy

Also known as NGC 224 and M31, the Andromeda Galaxy is a spiral galaxy that shares many characteristics with our own Milky Way Galaxy. Originally thought to be a component of the Milky Way, Andromeda was first mentioned as early as 964 CE by the Islamic scholar Abd Al-Rahman Al Sufi in his *Book of Fixed Stars*. It was rediscovered in 1612 by the German astronomer Simon Marius, who found it using the newly invented telescope. Originally thought to be a cloud of gas and dust, it was not until the 1920s that the astronomer Edwin Hubble showed that the Andromeda Galaxy is a separate galaxy in its own right lying beyond the boundaries of the Milky Way.

The Magellanic Clouds

Named after the Portuguese explorer Ferdinand Magellan, the Magellanic Clouds formed several billion years after the Milky Way Galaxy. Condensing from matter left over after the Big Bang, they contain many relatively young stars. This means that they provide an excellent opportunity for astronomers to study the formation and evolution of stars.

Back in 1987, the light from a supernova (exploding star) that had occurred 150,000 years ago finally reached us here on Earth, offering an unparalled opportunity to study the sudden death of a star that had previously been catalogued. This was the nearest supernova to Earth to occur in the last 200 years.

The Great Wall

Astronomers have identified a structure that is even larger than a supercluster. Called the Great Wall, it is made up of superclusters and a few scattered clusters. The Great Wall occupies a region of space measuring approximately 500 million light years by 300 million light years by 15 million light years. It is separated from the next 'wall' by an eerily empty region of space that spans some 400 million light years.

LEFT Large Magellanic Cloud, which is our nearest galactic neighbor.

Some galaxies in the Local Group

Name of galaxy	Distance in light years	Name of galaxy	Distance in light years
Milky Way	0	Andromeda II	2,200,000
Large Magellanic Cloud	179,000	Andromeda III	2,200,000
Small Magellanic Cloud	210,000	M32	2,200,000
Draco	300,000	NGC 147	2,200,000
Carina	300,000	NGC 185	2,200,000
Sculptor	300,000	NGC 205	2,200,000
Sextans	300,000	M33	2,400,000
Ursa Minor	300,000	IC 1613	2,500,000
Fornax	500,000	DDO 210	3,000,000
Leo I	600,000	Pisces	3,000,000
Leo II	600,000	GR8	4,000,000
NGC 6822	1,800,000	IC 10	4,000,000
IC 5152	2,000,000	Sagittarius	4,000,000
WLM	2,000,000	Pegasus	5,000,000
Andromeda	2,200,000	Leo A	5,000,000
Andromeda I	2,200,000		

FACT

Situated at a distance of 2.2 million light years from Earth, the Andromeda Galaxy is the most distant object that is visible to the naked eye. The galaxy was observed by Persian astronomers as far back as 905 CE, and was described by Abd-al-Rahman Al-Sufi in his 964 CE *Book of Fixed Stars* – he referred to it by the utterly charming name of "the little cloud."

Types of galaxies

In the 1920s Edwin Hubble defined galaxies according to types based on their appearance. These types were of four broad categories: irregular, elliptical, spiral and barred spiral. Advances in telescope and camera technology, in particular the use of the charge-coupled device (CCD) which "collects" light in a far more efficient way than the human eye could ever manage, means that we now have an unparalleled opportunity to view what are arguably the most magnificent structures in creation.

Irregular galaxies

Lacking any recognisable shape or structure, irregular galaxies tend to have less mass than other types of galaxies but are home to many bright young stars. Despite this, irregular galaxies make up less than five percent of the brightest thousand or so galaxies and yet form about a quarter of all known galaxies.

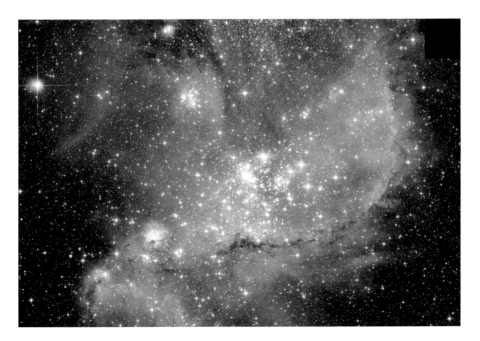

ABOVE An irregular-shaped galaxy, the Small Magellanic Cloud.

Elliptical galaxies

As the name suggests, elliptical galaxies are shaped like ellipses. The ellipse may be anything from almost spherical in shape to something approaching the shape of a football. Unlike the other types of galaxies, the elliptical galaxies appear yellow in color. This is because the process of star formation has generally all but stopped, which means that the stars in the galaxy are nearly all old red giant stars, tending for the most part to be more than 10 billion years old.

Barred spiral galaxies

In many respects similar to the spiral galaxies, barred spiral galaxies differ in one important detail: the bulging central nucleus is extended laterally in two directions to form a bar. This bar-shaped central nucleus can be a variety of sizes but the larger ones tend to have tightly wound arms while the smaller ones have arms that are loosely packed with stars. As the central bar rotates, the arms of the spiral appear to extend from each end of the bar. Although treated as a distinct type by Edwin Hubble, astronomers are increasingly beginning to recognize spiral and barred spiral galaxies as variations on the same theme.

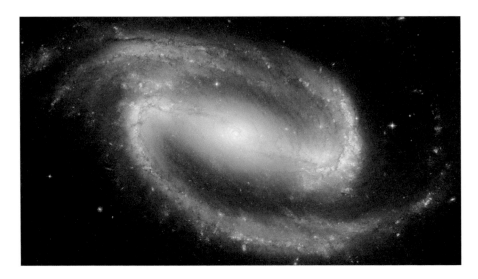

ABOVE An example of a barred spiral galaxy showing a bar of stars, dust and gas.

Spiral galaxies

Truly beautiful to behold, spiral galaxies are centered on a bulging nucleus from which extend several trailing arms of stars, from which they get their name. Older stars can be found in the dense nucleus with younger stars forming in the glowing pink nebulae of the far less dense arms. Vast amounts of gas and dust can also be found in the arms, some of which will ultimately condense to form new stars. The very oldest stars inhabit a sparsely populated "halo" which envelops the nucleus.

ABOVE The M100 galaxy is a large spiral galaxy similar to our own Milky Way, containing over 100 billion stars. It is over 150 million light years away. The picture was taken in 1993 with the Wide Field and Planetary Camera 2 onboard the Hubble Space Telescope.

When galaxies collide

It's tempting to think of galaxies as islands in space, fixed to a single spot around which they rotate. In reality, all the galaxies are flying through the Universe at tremendous speeds, with the galaxies furthest away from our own travelling fastest of all. Despite the vast distances separating galaxies – our nearest galactic neighbor is at least 170,000 light years away – galaxies occasionally collide . . . with results that go far beyond what might be described as catastrophic.

As two galaxies move closer together they become caught in each other's gravitational fields. Before long, visible streams of matter, initially nebulous gas and dust, can be seen pouring from one galaxy to the next. As this continues it has a dramatic effect on the appearance of the galaxies. Depending on the direction of drift the two galaxies may eventually merge to form a single, much more massive galaxy.

This is currently happening to galaxies NGC 4038 and NGC 4039, which together are known as the Antenna. Eventually, and inevitably, these two galaxies will combine to form a single galaxy.

Seyfert galaxies

Despite Edwin Hubble's best efforts, not all galaxies can be slotted into the four broad categories he defined. Since Hubble made his observations two other varieties of galaxy, each even more mysterious and exotic than anything known of before, have been discovered.

The first was recognized in 1943 by the American astronomer Carl K. Seyfert. When observing the spectral emissions for a number of apparently ordinary spiral galaxies, Seyfert noticed a concentration of hot gases, especially hydrogen, at their central cores. This gas was expanding at tremendous speed – up to several thousand miles (km) per second.

Despite appearing to be quite normal in conventional photographs, these galaxies were clearly very strong sources of infrared radiation. Many were also powerful sources of radio waves and X-rays, suggesting the presence of a huge black hole in the nucleus of the galaxy. Since Seyfert made his discovery astronomers have noticed that about one percent of all spiral galaxies are Seyfert galaxies. But it may yet prove to be the case that all spiral galaxies display Seyfert properties one percent of the time.

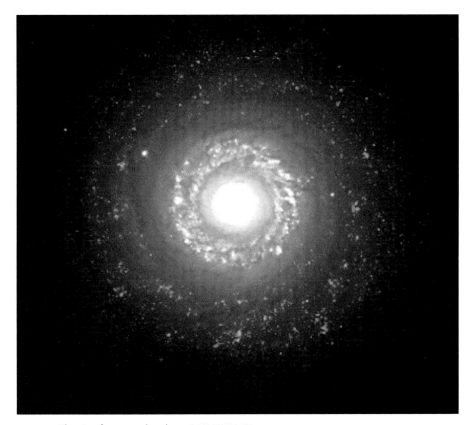

ABOVE The Seyfert spiral galaxy NGC 7742.

FACT
Not all stars are held in galaxies; some are roaming free throughout space. Using the Hubble Space Telescope, astronomers discovered over 600 stars adrift between the galaxies of the Virgo cluster.

FACT
Despite the remarkable amount of energy that is released
by these intense little galactic entities, no quasar is visible to
the naked eye – hardly surprising given their distance from
Earth. In addition to radio waves and light waves, quasars
are also powerful sources of X-rays, gamma rays, ultraviolet
light and infrared radiation.

Quasars

While Seyfert galaxies might be thought of as a specific type of spiral
galaxy, 1962 saw the discovery of a whole new – and truly ancient –
type of galactic entity. Thought to be related to Seyfert galaxies,
quasars are among the rarest and brightest objects in the Universe.

Classed as QSOs, which stands for "quasi-stellar objects" (the
name "quasar" is a shortening of "quasi-stellar radio source"), these
tiny galaxies are never more than a couple of light years across yet
shine a thousand times brighter than galaxies with a diameter of over
100,000 light years.

The incomparable brilliance of the quasar means that they can be
observed from Earth despite being up to 10 billion light years away.
The enormous amounts of radiation required for such a feat are
released from just a small area at the center of the quasar. Many
astronomers believe that this energy is being released by gases
accelerating to speeds approaching those of light as they are sucked
into a supermassive black hole.

The brightest quasar so far discovered is also the nearest one to
us. Situated two billion light years from Earth, NGC 3C 273 has
a nucleus that is currently expanding at very near the speed of light,
a fact which points to the presence of a black hole at the center of
this quasar. Quasars are so bright that some can be observed even
though the energy coming from them began its journey to us five
billion years before our Sun was born.

SPACE
EXPLORATION

How rockets work

A rocket engine is really just a firework built on a grand scale. It requires fuel, which might be liquid hydrogen, and a source of oxygen, the gas needed for combustion. This mixture of fuel and oxidizer is known as the propellant and it is burned to produce hot gases which expand rapidly. This rapidly expanding gas is forced through a nozzle at the base of the rocket in order to propel it in an upwards direction.

This is not a new idea. The Chinese were making rockets – for military and display purposes – as early as the eleventh century. The principle on which the rocket lifts off the ground and continues its journey skywards was described by the English scientist Isaac Newton in the seventeenth century. His Third Law of Motion states that for every action (the downward thrust of the gases) there is an equal and opposite reaction (lift–off).

Once a rocket has left the ground it relies on the thrust from the gas propellant to carry on climbing upwards. The rate of climb depends on the amount of thrust the rocket engines produce and the mass of the rocket itself – the more the rocket weighs the more thrust it needs to travel the 50 miles (80 km) or so into space. The rocket will continue to accelerate for just as long as the rocket engines are burning.

Types of rocket engine

Rocket engines are of two main types: solid fuel or liquid propellant. Some, such as the space shuttle, may be equipped with both for take-off. As an alternative, extremely efficient nuclear-powered rockets have been proposed. But so far fears over the consequences of an accident occurring with such an engine have kept this scheme at the drawing-board stage.

RIGHT Space shuttle *Atlantis* leaps from the steam and smoke billowing across Launch Pad 39B after an on-time lift-off of 3:46 p.m. EDT on mission STS-112.

Early rocketry

As far back as 1903 the Russian scientist Konstantin Tsiolkovsky suggested that rockets which use liquid propellants could reach space. This may not seem like an especially significant suggestion but it was the first seriously proposed change to the design of rockets to have occurred in nearly 900 years.

After much work and many failures, a successful design for a liquid fuel rocket was demonstrated in 1926 by the American scientist Robert Goddard. But it was the onset of war, however, that provided the impetus – and

ABOVE Robert Goddard with an early rocket design which he hoped would provide greater stability in flight.

an enormous injection of funding – required to build rockets that had the power to reach into outer space.

Von Braun and the *V2*

In 1944 the German military launched a terrible new weapon on the cities of Paris, Antwerp and London. Travelling faster than the speed of sound – and so arriving before anyone could be warned of its approach – the *V2* rocket was able to carry a 2,200-pound (1,000-kg) warhead over a distance of 200 miles (320 km) and, most significantly, at a height of up to 100 miles (160 km). Germany may have failed in its bid to conquer the world, but as part of its war effort it had conquered space. The man who led the team that developed the *V2* rocket at Peenemünde in Germany was Werner von Braun. At the end of the war he surrendered to American forces and went on to develop the *Saturn V* rocket, an essential part of the *Apollo* program that culminated in the successful Moon landing of 1969.

Korolyov and the Soviets

The most important figure in the early decades of the space age was a little-known Ukrainian-born engineer called Sergei Korolyov. He was responsible for the development of all Soviet spacecraft up to and including the *Soyuz* series and played a vital role in the launch of *Sputnik 1*, the first satellite in space. He also guided the first human spaceflight (by Yuri Gagarin in 1961) and the first spacewalk (by Aleksei Leonov in 1965).

BELOW Evolution of Soviet rockets.

| Test vehicle | *Sputnik* launcher | *Vostok* launcher | *Voskhod* launcher | *Soyuz* launcher |

49.3 ft

44.5 ft

38.3 ft

34.2 ft

29.2 ft

50

40

30

20

10

0

Meters

FACT
The first satellite in space was called *Sputnik*. The word is Russian for "travelling companion," or "satellite."

Timeline of rocketry and space exploration

Date	Event
c.1100	China develops the first rockets, essentially large fireworks which are used for military and display purposes.
c.1700	Rocket technology rediscovered in the West; rockets appear on European battlefields.
c.1792	Indian prince Tipu Sultan uses a new and more powerful rocket against the British at Seringapatam.
c.1810	Artillery officer William Congreve improves on the design of the rockets he saw first-hand at Seringapatam, building one that will travel over 1,650 feet (2,000 m) to its target. His rockets are used to attack Boulogne, Copenhagen and Danzig during the Napoleonic Wars and in the British attack on Fort McHenry, in Baltimore, during the War of 1812.
c.1850	British engineer William Hale eliminates the deadweight of the flight-stabilizing guide stick (a feature of previous rocket designs) by adding jet vents at an angle which make the rocket spin, thus stabilizing its flight through the air.
1861–65	Rockets are used with varying degrees of success during the Civil War.
c.1900	Swedish engineer Wilhelm Unge invents an "aerial torpedo," which is designed to be used as a surface-to-air weapon against dirigibles.
1915	Konstantin Tsiolkovsky designs, but does not build, the first liquid-fuel rocket.
1920s	Amateur rocket-enthusiast clubs open up all over Europe and the United States.
1930s	The military assumes control of the main rocket clubs in Germany.
1944	The German military launch the *V2* rocket weapon against Paris, Antwerp and London.
c.1945	The USSR and the USA begin the race to build rockets capable of carrying nuclear weapons.
Oct 1957	The USSR successfully launches *Sputnik 1*, the first artificial satellite in space.
Nov 1957	The USSR's *Sputnik 2* mission puts a dog, Laika, into space. The animal dies shortly after take-off from overheating and stress.

Date	Event
Jan 1959	USSR's *Luna 1* mission escapes Earth's gravity.
Sep 1959	*Luna 2* reaches the Moon.
July 1959	*Luna 3* photographs the far side of the Moon.
May 1960	*ECHO 1*, the first communications satellite, is launched by the United States.
Jan 31, 1961	A chimpanzee named "Ham" is sent into space and returned alive as part of the US *Mercury* program.
April 12, 1961	Yuri Gagarin becomes the first man in space.
May 5, 1961	Alan Shepard becomes the first American in space.
Feb 20, 1962	John Glenn becomes the first American to orbit the Earth.
June 16, 1963	Valentina Tereshkova becomes the first woman in space.
Mar 18, 1965	Soviet cosmonaut Alexei Leonov makes the first spacewalk.
1966	The USSR lands a spacecraft on the surface of Venus.
Dec 21-27, 1968	The crew of *Apollo 8* orbit the Moon.
July 20, 1969	*Apollo 11* astronauts Neil Armstrong and Buzz Aldrin become the first men to set foot on the Moon. Fellow crew member, Michael Collins, remains in orbit around the Moon.
April 19, 1971	The Soviets launch the first space station, *Salyut 1*.
Nov 27, 1971	The Soviets crash-land a probe on Mars.
1981	The United States launches the space shuttle.
1990	The Hubble Space Telescope is launched.
2000	The International Space Station opens for business.

FACT

Francis Scott Key described "the rockets' red glare, the bombs bursting in air" during the British attack on Fort McHenry in "The Star–Spangled Banner," which would later became the American national anthem.

BELOW Map of the world's launch sites.

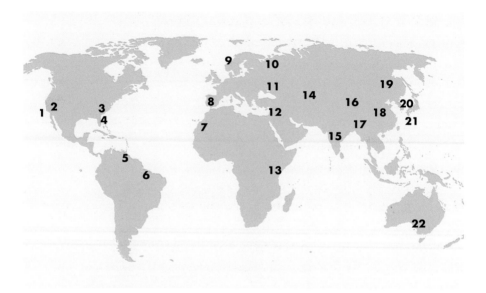

1	Vandenberg, USA	12	Palmachim, Israel
2	Edwards, USA	13	San Marco, Kenya
3	Wallops Island, USA	14	Baikonur, Russia
4	Cape Canaveral, USA	15	Sriharikota, India
5	Kourou, French Guiana	16	Jiuquan, China
6	Alcantara, Brazil	17	Xichang, China
7	Hammaguir, Algeria	18	Taiyuan, China
8	Torrejon, Spain	19	Svobodny, Russia
9	Andoya, Norway	20	Kagoshima, Japan
10	Plesetsk, Russia	21	Tanegashima, Japan
11	Kapustin Yar, Russia	22	Woomera, Australia

Launch sites are few and far between with some open to the public, while others remain top-secret. The locations for spaceports are decided according to both political and technical realities. The most used ports are Cape Canaveral, Vandenberg, Baikonur, Plesetsk, Kourou, Tanegashima, Jiuquan, Xichang and Sriharikota.

Competition for the world's largest space program remains intense, with the United States and Russia heading the race, followed by the ESA (European Space Agency), France, Japan, Germany, Italy, India, the United Kingdom, Canada, Brazil, Belgium and Spain.

The space race

World War II saw the rise of two superpowers, the USSR and the United States. In the aftermath of the war, each competed with the other to build evermore sophisticated rockets capable of carrying nuclear weapons to the enemy's territory. Initially, and by virtue of superior design, the USSR led the way. In 1957, they succeeded in placing the first artificial satellite in space and topped this remarkable feat in 1961 by launching cosmonaut Yuri Gagarin on a trajectory that took him, briefly, into space.

By now, the United States was losing face and everyone knew it. Fearing the potential of unstoppable space-based weapons systems, the United States began to pour money into research and development. Faced with the need for a face-saving exercise in the wake of the disastrous Bay of Pigs incident of 1961, US President John F. Kennedy pledged to place a man on the Moon before the end of the decade. On July 20, 1969 Neil Armstrong left the very first human footprint on the Moon and uttered the immortal line, "That's one small step for a man, one giant leap for mankind." At the final hurdle, the USSR had lost the space race.

ABOVE JFK dedicating his nation to the race to space.

FACT
Because there is no atmosphere on the Moon, Neil Armstrong's first footsteps will not blow away. They are preserved in the dust that covers the Moon's surface and will remain there until someone – or something – in the future erases them.

ABOVE Yuri Gagarin on the Vostok 1 flight on April 12, 1961.

Vostok

Between April 1961 and 1963 the USSR launched six manned missions to Earth orbit as part of the *Vostok* program. The first of these missions saw Yuri Gagarin become the first human in space. *Vostok 2* made 17.5 orbits of the Earth. *Vostok 3* and *Vostok 4* were launched together and orbited within sight of each other. *Vostok 5* was launched on June 14, 1963 followed two days later by *Vostok 6*, which carried the first woman cosmonaut, Valentina Tereshkova, into space.

Mercury

Mercury, the US answer to the *Vostok* program, had its first official launch on May 5, 1961, when Mercury 3 took Alan Shephard on a suborbital flight lasting 15 minutes and 22 seconds. The flight of *Mercury 4*, carrying Virgil "Gus" Grissom and launched the same year lasted an extra 15 seconds. *Mercury 5* launched in November 1961 and was an orbital flight crewed by a chimpanzee. *Mercury 6* followed in February 1962 with John Glenn at the controls. *Mercury 7* and *Mercury 8* followed in May and October of that year with the final flight of the program launching in May 1963.

ABOVE *Project Mercury* astronauts, September 13, 1968.

Project Gemini

Between 1963 and 1966 the United States launched 10 two-man missions into Earth orbit in a 12-stage project known as *Gemini*. The project was designed to test the ability of astronauts to maneuver themselves and their equipment in the weightless environment of space. It also helped NASA to develop the techniques needed for orbital rendezvous and docking, procedures that were to play a vital role in the subsequent *Apollo* mission to the Moon.

Gemini 1 & 2. *In 1964 and 1965, NASA launched two preliminary spacecrafts to test that all the technology functioned properly. Both launches were successful.*

Gemini 3. *Launching on March 23, 1965, this was the first US spacecraft to carry two men into space.*

Gemini 4. *This was launched on a four-day mission on June 3, 1965. It was during this flight that US astronaut Ed White became the first American to walk in space: he left the* **Gemini** *capsule for 22 minutes.*

Gemini 5. *Its crew set a new record when it orbited the Earth for nearly eight days starting on August 21, 1965.*

Gemini 6. *The launch vehicle exploded on take-off but finally achieved orbit on December 15, 1965.*

Gemini 7. *This reached space on December 4, 1965.*

Gemini 8. *Piloted by Neil Armstrong,* **Gemini 8** *achieved the first successful space docking after it was launched on March 16, 1966.*

Gemini 9. *On June 3, 1966* **Gemini 9** *reached space where astronaut Eugene "Gene" Cernan, later the last man to walk on the Moon, took his first walk in space.*

Gemini 10. *This launched without incident on July 18, 1966.*

Gemini 11. *Launched on September 12, 1966.*

Gemini 12. *The last mission of the* **Gemini** *program was launched on November 11, 1966. The way to the Moon was now clear and would be achieved via a new set of missions: the* **Apollo** *project.*

LEFT Gemini-Titan 4 launch. The flight included the first space walk by a US astronaut on March 6, 1965.

Significant Space Missions

Date	Name (nationality)	Mission objective	Mission outcome
October 4, 1957	*Sputnik 1* (USSR)	First Earth orbiter.	Successfully completed.
November 3, 1957	*Sputnik 2* (USSR)	First Earthling in space: Laika the dog!	Died after a week in space.
April 12, 1961	*Vostok 1* (USSR)	First man in space. Yuri Gagarin orbited Earth once.	Successfully completed.
June 16, 1963	*Vostok 6* (USSR)	First woman in space: Valentina Tereshkova.	Successfully completed.
March 18, 1965	*Voskhod 2* (USSR)	First spacewalk: Alexei Leonov.	Successfully completed.
August 17, 1970	*Venera 7* (USSR)	First Venus lander.	Successfully completed.
May 14, 1973	*Skylab* (USA)	Space station (carried the first toilet and first shower in space).	After successfully completing mission brief, burned up in atmosphere.
August 20, 1975	*Viking 1* (USA)	Martian lander.	Successfully completed.
April 12, 1981	*STS-1 Space Shuttle Columbia* (USA)	First shuttle mission: systems check.	Successfully completed.
July 2, 1985	*Giotto* (Europe)	Visited Halley's Comet.	Successfully completed.
January 28, 1986	*STS-51-L Space Shuttle Challenger* (USA)	Deployment of tracking satellite and Halley's Comet observer.	Exploded on launch, all astronauts lost.
September 25, 1992	*Mars Observer* (USA)	Mars orbiter.	Contact lost.
December 4, 1996	*Mars Pathfinder* (USA)	Mars lander and rover.	Successful.
January 3, 1999	*Mars Polar Lander* (USA)	Mars lander.	Mission failure.
January 16, 2003	*STS-107 Space Shuttle Columbia* (USA)	16-day mission dedicated to research in physical, life and space sciences.	Exploded on re-entry, all astronauts lost.

The *Apollo* program

January 27, 1967 should have marked the day that the *Apollo* program finally left the launch pad. As *Apollo 1* sat on the launch pad its crew, Virgil "Gus" Grissom, Edward White and Roger Chafee, carried out last-minute checks of the craft's command systems. By now the three men, who had been sealed into the cramped capsule, were breathing an atmosphere of pure oxygen and praying that nothing would go wrong.

A single spark triggered an electrical fire. In the pressurized pure-oxygen atmosphere of the capsule there was no way of stopping the blaze. In seconds all three men were engulfed in the blowtorch blaze with no hope of escape or rescue. By the time they were freed from the seats in which they had died, their bodies had been burned beyond recognition, victims of bad design and even worse luck. The next *Apollo* capsule would have an escape hatch.

The stated aim of the *Apollo* program was to place a man on the Moon before the end of the 1960s. At the time the announcement was made only two people had ever travelled into space, and even then for only a few minutes in total. But by the time that the crew of *Apollo 1* approached their vehicle for take-off a good deal of groundwork had been carried out, with first American one-man (*Mercury* program) and then two-man (*Gemini* program) vehicles taking to space in what were essentially preparatory flights for the journey to the Moon.

After the *Apollo 1* disaster the next two flights were cancelled. Finally, test flights for the *Apollo* program began again on November 9, 1967 with the launch of *Apollo 4*.

The *Apollo* Missions

Apollo 1

Launch date: January 27, 1967

Astronauts Virgil Grissom, Edward White and Roger Chafee all died tragically when an electrical fire broke out on the spacecraft just before take-off.

Apollo 4
Launch date: November 9, 1967

The *Apollo* program resumed with an unmanned mission which saw NASA test the first *Apollo-Saturn V* rocket combination in flight.

Apollo 5
Launch date: January 22, 1968

This unmanned mission saw the first test flight, in Earth orbit, of the Lunar Module (the part of the craft that would eventually land on the Moon).

Apollo 6
Launch date: April 4, 1968

The final unmanned mission saw further testing of the *Saturn V* rocket that would eventually send the *Apollo* spacecraft to the Moon.

Apollo 7
Launch date: October 11, 1968

Astronauts Walter Schirra, Walter Cunningham and Donn Eisele tested and evaluated *Apollo's* navigation and control systems over the course of 11 days while in Earth orbit.

Apollo 8
Launch date: December 21, 1968

The crew of *Apollo 8* – Frank Borman, James Lovell and William Anders – became the first people in history to escape Earth's gravity. They went on to fly around the Moon, orbiting it 10 times on Christmas Eve 1968 while observing possible landing sites for later *Apollo* missions.

Apollo 9
Launch date: March 3, 1969

Astronauts James McDivitt, David Scott and Russell Schwieckart orbited the Earth 152 times while testing out docking procedures and the *Apollo* Life Support System, a specially designed space suit.

Apollo 10

Launch date: May 18, 1969

Essentially a full dress rehearsal for the actual Moon landing, astronaut Thomas Stafford remained in orbit around the Moon while John Young and Eugene Cernan flew the *Lunar Module* to within 9 miles (15 km) of the surface of the Moon, all the while resisting the tremendous urge to land the craft and enter the history books as the first men on the Moon.

Apollo 11

Launch date: July 16, 1969

The big one! On July 20, 1969 an estimated one billion people were glued to their TV sets, witnesses to the remarkable sight of astronaut Neil Armstrong taking his first steps on the Moon and uttering one of the most famous (and famously misquoted) lines in history: "That's one small step for a man; one giant leap for mankind." He was followed on to the surface of the Moon some 20 or so minutes later by Buzz Aldrin, who never really got over the disappointment of being the second man on the Moon. The other astronaut, Michael Collins, remained in orbit while history unfolded beneath him.

Apollo 12

Launch date: November 14, 1969

Astronauts Charles Conrad and Alan Bean spent nearly 32 hours on the Moon where they collected samples and carried out experiments before blasting off to rejoin Richard Gordon in orbit around the Moon in the command module. They arrived back at Earth on November 24.

ABOVE *Apollo 11* bootprint for Buzz Aldrin on July 20, 1969.

FACT
Although an estimated one billion people watched the Moon landing, by the end of the *Apollo 12* mission viewers all over Europe and America were phoning in to complain that their regular soap operas were being disrupted by coverage of events on the Moon.

Apollo 13

Launch date: April 11, 1970

At about 1:00 p.m. on April 13, *Apollo 13* suffered disaster when an oxygen tank exploded in the service module. More than halfway to the Moon, the crew of James Lovell, John Swigert and Fred Haise found themselves trapped in the icy cold depths of space with no possibility of rescue aboard a ship that could no longer supply them with power, oxygen or water. Surviving on the Lunar Module's limited supply of oxygen, the men managed to return to Earth relatively unharmed despite the appalling conditions onboard. They splashed down in the Pacific Ocean on April 17, 1970.

ABOVE *Apollo 13* view of damaged service module.

Apollo 14
Launch date: January 31, 1971

Astronauts Alan Shepard and Edgar Mitchell landed safely on the Moon and carried out many of the experiments that had originally been part of the *Apollo 13* mission. Stuart Roosa remained in orbit around the Moon.

Apollo 15
Launch date: July 26, 1971

As part of the first mission that used the *Lunar Roving Vehicle*, astronauts David Scott and James Irwin drove across nearly 17.5 miles (28 km) of the Moon's surface while conducting detailed studies of the area. Meanwhile, astronaut Alfred Worden remained in orbit around the Moon.

Apollo 16
Launch date: April 16, 1972

Astronauts John Young and Charles Duke took core samples and seismic soundings during the 20 hours they spent outside the *Lunar Module*. Meanwhile, astronaut Thomas Mattingly remained in orbit around the Moon so that he could work on mapping the pitted surface.

Apollo 17
Launch date: December 7, 1972

Astronauts Harrison "Jack" Schmitt and Eugene Cernan were the last men to walk on the Moon as part of a sample-gathering mission which saw them travel over 19 miles (30 km) across the surface of the Moon in the *Lunar Rover*. Astronaut Ronald Evans remained in orbit around the Moon.

Space stations

Placed in high orbit around the Earth, space stations are essentially little more than science labs with spectacular views. Some provision is made for the crew, but, distinctly Spartan accommodation aside,

FACT
The very first space shuttle was named *Enterprise* in honor of the spaceship in the television series *Star Trek*. Although it never made it into orbit, it was being used for test landings as far back as 1977.

these vehicles offer an unparalleled opportunity to conduct experiments in a weightless environment that is also free from the effects of the Earth's atmosphere.

Solar panels are an obvious feature of all space stations, generating electricity to power essential systems while reducing the need for heavy battery packs. Shielding protects the crew from the worst effects of solar radiation and space debris and a docking port allows supply craft to deliver cargo. This also means that the crew of the space station can be replaced without the vessel having to return to Earth.

In the future scientists have suggested placing space stations outside of Earth orbit so that they can act as convenient rest and re-supply stops on the journey to planets such a Mars and, perhaps, beyond.

ABOVE *Salyut 2* series space station.

The space shuttle

Launched in 1981, the space shuttle was a revolutionary craft: it was the first-ever reusable space ship. The design of the shuttle breaks down into three principal components, the orbiter space plane (the part most people think of when they imagine the shuttle), huge solid-fuel rocket boosters and an external fuel tank. Of these three components only the fuel tank is not reused after a flight.

Once in space, the shuttle is maneuvered between orbits, the altitude of which can be up to 244 miles (390 km), using the orbital maneuvering system at the rear of the craft. Smaller movements are effected using tiny jets.

A large robotic device called the remote manipulator arm is used to move the shuttle's payload, which might be a satellite, into space or to collect it for repair or recovery. Alternatively, the payload bay can be fitted with *Spacelab*, a special laboratory designed and built by the European Space Agency for use in Earth orbit.

ABOVE Looking down into the payload of the space shuttle in flight.

Satellites

For our purposes a satellite is an object that sits in orbit around Earth. It was the launch of a satellite, the tiny *Sputnik 1*, which triggered the space race. In July 1955, the White House declared its intention to launch a satellite into the Earth's orbit by the spring of 1958, only to be beaten to it by the Soviet Union, which launched *Sputnik 1* on October 4, 1957. Over the next decade or so, the United States responded by investing trillions of dollars in order to regain supremacy in space, and while much of it was invested in high-profile manned missions to the Moon, more than a little was spent on the far less glamorous, but much more practical, satellite program.

Military satellites are designed for monitoring and communication purposes, such as GPS (Global Positioning System) signals and the guidance of "Smart" missiles to their targets. The first commercial satellites were developed in order to aid communication, providing the opportunity to broadcast signals reliably beyond the horizon by bouncing them off an object fixed in orbit around Earth. Most communications satellites are held in high geostationary orbits where they enable everything from television broadcasts to long-distance telephone conversations.

Types of orbits	Distance above Earth's surface
Low Earth Orbit (LEO)	124–746 miles (200–1,200 km)
Medium Earth Orbit (MEO)	746–21,927 miles (1,200–35,286 km)
Geosynchronus Orbit (GEO)	22,237 miles (35,786 km)
High Earth Orbit (HEO)	22,237+ miles (35,786+ km))

FACT
The largest artificial satellite in orbit around Earth is the International Space Station.

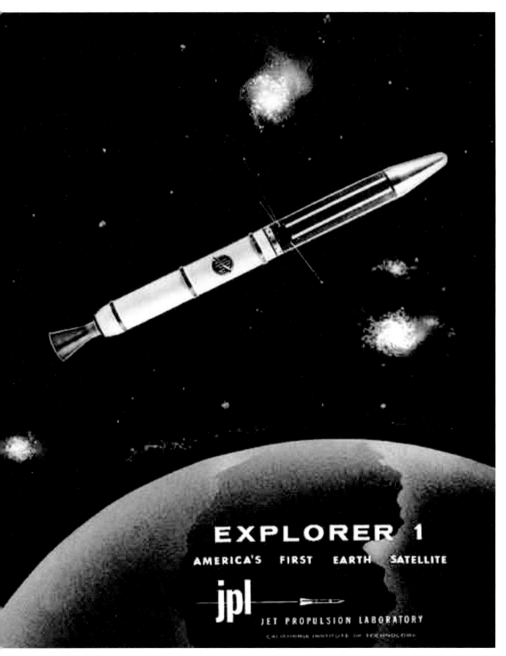

ABOVE *Explorer 1*, the first US satellite, successfully launched on January 31, 1958.

FACT
The geostationary orbit (also known as the Clarke Orbit) is the brainchild of science fiction writer Arthur C. Clarke. In 1945, he suggested that a satellite could be made to orbit the Earth at the same speed as Earth rotates on its axis, effectively fixing the satellite over one spot on the planet.

Probes

Probes, although often similar in size to satellites, are unmanned spacecraft designed to carry cameras and monitoring equipment beyond Earth's orbit to distant planets and moons. Once there, the probe can be controlled remotely, or simply follow a pre-programmed set of instructions, making whatever observations are necessary before broadcasting the information back in the form of radio waves to receiving stations here on Earth.

The earliest successful probe was the Soviet Union's *Luna 1*, which reached the surface of the Moon in 1959 – a full ten years before the United States landed a man on the surface.

Arguably, the most successful probe so far has been *Pioneer 10*, which was launched by NASA on March 2, 1972. Originally designed to observe Jupiter, it became the first man-made object to leave the Solar System when, in 1983, it passed beyond the orbit of Pluto and into a region of space that still remains a mystery.

Scientists finally abandoned the probe after it became apparent that its last signal had been received on January 22, 2003. At the time of broadcast, the probe was approximately 7.6 billion miles (12 billion km) away and its signal, which was travelling at the speed of light, took eleven hours and twenty minutes to reach Earth.

Probes designed to explore our Solar System can be powered using solar panels. Those going far from the Sun, however, require electricity generated using the heat from radioactive materials.

Lunar probes	Function
Luna program	Soviet lunar exploration (1959–1976).
Ranger program	US lunar hard-landing probes (1961–1965).
Zond program	Soviet lunar exploration (1964–1970).
Surveyor program	US lunar soft-landing probe (1966–1968).
Lunar Orbiter program	US lunar orbital (1966–1967).
Lunokhod program	Soviet lunar Rover probes (1970–1973).
Muses-A mission (*Hiten* and *Hagoromo*)	Japanese lunar orbital and hard-landing probes (1990–1993).
Clementine	US lunar orbital (1998).
Lunar Prospector	US lunar orbital (1998–1999).
Smart 1	European lunar orbital (2003).
Kaguya	Japanese lunar orbiter and lander (2007–2009).
Lunar Atmosphere and Dust Environment Explorer (LADEE)	US lunar orbital (2013–2014).

Mars probes	Function
Mars probe program	Soviet orbiters and landers (1960–1988).
Viking program	Two US orbiters and landers (1974).
Phobos program	Failed Soviet orbiters (1988–1989).
Mars Pathfinder	Lander and wheeled robot (1996–1997).
Mars Odyssey	US orbiter (launched 2001).
Mars Express Orbiter and *Beagle 2*	European orbiter and failed lander (launched 2003).
Mars Exploration Rovers	US rovers (launched 2003).
Mars Reconnaissance Orbiter	US orbiter (launched 2005).
Mars Science Laboratory	US rover (launched 2011).
Mars Atmosphere and Volatile Evolution (MAVEN)	US orbiter (launched 2013)

Other Space Missions

Launch date	Mission name	Mission objective
November 3, 1973	Mariner 10 (USA)	Mercury and Venus flyby.
August 20, 1977	Voyager 1 (USA)	Jupiter and Saturn flyby.
September 5, 1977	Voyager 2 (USA)	Jupiter, Saturn, Uranus and Neptune flyby.
October 18, 1989	Galileo (USA)	Orbiting Jupiter.
April 25, 1990	Hubble Telescope (USA)	First and flagship mission of NASA's Great Observatories program.
October 15, 1997	Cassini (USA)	Orbital survey of Saturn.
October 15, 1997	Huygens (ESA) (onboard Cassini)	Landing on Titan.
June 30, 2001	Wilkinson Microwave Anisotropy Probe (USA)	Measuring the Cosmic Microwave Background (CMB), left over from the Big Bang.
May 9, 2003	Hayabusa (Japan)	Landing on the asteroid Itokawa and bringing samples back to Earth.
August 25, 2003	Spitzer Space Telescope (USA)	Using infrared technology to study far-off objects that would not otherwise be seen.
February 26, 2004	Rosetta (ESA)	Orbitial survey of the comet 67P/Churyumov–Gerasimenko.
August 3, 2004	MESSENGER (USA)	Orbital survey of Mercury.
January 11, 2005	Venus Express (ESA)	Orbital survey of Venus.
September 27, 2007	Dawn (USA)	Orbital survey of Vesta and Ceres.
January 19, 2006	New Horizons (USA)	Flyby of Pluto and its moons.
March 7, 2009	Kepler (USA) planet finder	Searching for Earth-like exoplanets.
January 1, 2011	BepiColombo (ESA)	Orbital survey of Mercury.
August 5, 2011	Juno (USA)	Orbital survey of Jupiter.

ABOVE *Viking 2* on Mars' Utopian plain, September 3, 1976.

Glossary

absolute magnitude A measure of how bright an object is, no matter how it appears from Earth.

apparent magnitude A measure of how bright an object appears from Earth.

bacteria A group of very small, single-celled living things.

black hole An object that has such a strong gravitational pull that not even light can escape it.

electromagnetic force The force that causes interaction between electrically charged particles.

electrons Tiny particles of matter that have negative electric charges and travel around an atom's nucleus.

ellipse A closed curved plane, the boundaries of which can be generated by a point moving in such a way that the sums of its distances from two fixed points is constant.

gravity The force that causes objects with matter to be drawn toward each other.

heliocentric Having the Sun as the center.

hemisphere Half of a sphere, in particular, half of the Earth.

heretical Having a belief or opinion that is contrary to the belief or opinion of a particular religion.

light year A unit of length equal to the distance that light can travel in one year.

nebula A cloud of dust and gas in space. The plural of nebula is nebulae.

neutrons Tiny particles of matter that have no electric charges and are part of the nuclei of most atoms.

nuclear fusion The joining of atomic nuclei to form heavier nuclei, which causes huge amounts of energy to be released.

nucleus The central part of an atom. It is made up of protons and neutrons. The plural of nucleus is nuclei.

protons Tiny particles of matter that have positive electric charges and are part of the nuclei of all atoms.

strong nuclear force The force that holds the particles in the nucleus of an atom together. Also known as the strong interaction.

vacuum An empty space where there is no air or other gas.

weak interaction A force that causes radioactive decay. It is also known as the weak nuclear force.

For More Information

Astronomical League
Astronomical League National Headquarters
9201 Ward Parkway; Suite 100
Kansas City, MO 64114
(816) 333-7759
Website: http://www.astroleague.org
This organization is comprised of more than 250 astronomical societies from across the United States. It represents more than 15,000 amateur astronomers. The group holds conferences and sponsors Astronomy Days to spread interest in astronomy.

Canadian Space Agency (CSA)
John H. Chapman Space Centre
6767 Route de l'Aéroport
Saint-Hubert, Quebec J3Y 8Y9
Canada
(450) 926-4800
Website: http://www.asc-csa.gc.ca/eng/default.asp
Established in 1989, the CSA carries out research and promotes greater knowledge about space. Important facilities include the John H. Chapman Space Centre, in Quebec, and David Florida Laboratory, in Ottawa.

European Space Agency (ESA)
ESA HQ Mario-Nikis
8-10 rue Mario Nikis
75738 Paris Cedex 15
France
+33 1 53 69 76 54
Website: http://www.esa.int/ESA
Established in 1964, the ESA serves as the joint space agency for several different European nations. It coordinates the space programs of its member nations and has been involved in many space missions.

International Astronomical Union (IAU)
IAU - UAI Secretariat
98-bis Blvd Arago
F–75014 Paris
France
+33 (0) 1 43 25 83 58
Website: http://www.iau.org
This international organization of professional astronomers from
   around the world was formed in 1919. It promotes astronomical
   research and educates the public about astronomical discoveries.
   At meetings that take place every three years, scientists establish
   scientific definitions and agree on the naming of objects in space.

National Aeronautics and Space Administration (NASA)
Public Communications Office
NASA Headquarters Suite 2R40
Washington, DC 20546
(202) 358-0001
Website: http://www.nasa.gov
Established in 1959, NASA is the space agency of US government. It
   does scientific research on a wide range of space-related topics,
   carries out both manned and unmanned missions, and has long
   been a world leader in space exploration.

National Air and Space Museum
600 Independence Avenue SW
Washington, DC 20560
(202) 633-2214
Website: http://airandspace.si.edu
This museum is part of the Smithsonian Institution, which is the
   world's largest museum and research complex. The Smithsonian
   was founded in 1846, while the National Air and Space
   Museum opened in 1976. It puts on exhibitions on aviation,
   space exploration, and planetary science.

Rose Center for Earth and Space
American Museum of Natural History
Central Park West at 79th Street
New York, NY 10024
(212) 769-5100
Website: http://www.amnh.org/exhibitions/permanent-exhibitions
    /rose-center-for-earth-and-space
This division of the American Natural History Museum has many
    programs to help visitors learn about space. It contains the
    Hayden Planetarium, which first opened in 1935 and has been
    educating the public about space ever since.

Royal Astronomical Society of Canada
203-4920 Dundas Street W
Toronto, ON M9A 1B7
Canada
(416) 924-7973
Website: https://www.rasc.ca
This organization is made up a mix of professional astronomers,
    amateur astronomers, and educators. It was founded in 1868 and
    now has local chapters across the country.

Websites

Because of the changing nature of Internet links, Rosen Publishing has
developed an online list of websites related to the subject of this book.
This site is updated regularly. Please use this link to access this list:

http://www.rosenlinks.com/GCM/Outer

For Further Reading

Benson, Michael. *Far Out: A Space-Time Chronicle.* New York, NY: Harry N. Abrams, 2009.

Chaisson, Eric, and Steve McMillan. *Astronomy: A Beginner's Guide to the Universe.* Boston, MA: Addison-Wesley, 2012.

Chown, Marcus. *Solar System: A Visual Exploration of All the Planets, Moons and Other Heavenly Bodies that Orbit Our Sun.* New York, NY: Black Dog & Leventhal Publishers, 2011.

Consolmagno, Guy, and Dan M. Davis. *Turn Left at Orion: Hundreds of Night Sky Objects to See in a Home Telescope – and How to Find Them.* New York, NY: Cambridge University Press, 2011.

Devorkin, David, and Robert Smith. *Hubble: Imaging Space and Time.* London, England: National Geographic, 2011.

Dickinson, Terence. *Hubble's Universe: Greatest Discoveries and Latest Images.* Richmond Hill, ON: Firefly Books, 2012.

French, Sue. *Deep-Sky Wonders: A Tour of the Universe with Sky and Telescope's Sue French.* Richmond Hill, ON: Firefly Books, 2011.

Graham, Ian. *What Do We Know About the Solar System?* (Earth, Space, & Beyond). North Mankato, MN: Raintree Freestyle Express, 2011.

Greenstein, George. *Understanding the Universe: An Inquiry Approach to Astronomy and the Nature of Scientific Research.* New York, NY: Cambridge University Press, 2013.

Gregersen, Erik, ed. *Astronomical Observations: Astronomy and the Study of Deep Space.* New York, NY: Rosen Educational Services, 2010.

Hirshfeld, Alan. *Starlight Detectives: How Astronomers, Inventors, and Eccentrics Discovered the Modern Universe.* New York, NY: Bellevue Literary Press, 2014.

Hollar, Sherman. *The Outer Planets: Jupiter, Saturn, Uranus, and Neptune.* (Solar System). New York, NY: Rosen Educational Services, 2011.

Impey, Chris, and Holly Henry. *Dreams of Other Worlds: The Amazing Story of Unmanned Space Exploration.* Princeton, NJ: Princeton University Press, 2013.

May, Brian, Patrick Moore, and Chris Lintott. *Bang!: The Complete History of the Universe*. 4th Edition. New York, NY: Carlton Books, 2013.

North, John. *Cosmos: An Illustrated History of Astronomy and Cosmology*. Chicago, IL: University of Chicago Press, 2008.

Panek, Richard. *The 4 Percent Universe: Dark Matter, Dark Energy, and the Race to Discover the Rest of Reality*. Wilmington, MA: Mariner Books, 2011.

Pyle, Rod. *Curiosity: An Inside Look at the Mars Rover Mission and the People Who Made It Happen*. Amherst, NY: Prometheus Books, 2014.

Sivolella, Davide. *To Orbit and Back Again: How the Space Shuttle Flew in Space*. New York: Springer, 2013.

Than, Ker. *Black Holes* (True Books: Space). New York, NY: Scholastic, 2010.

Trefil, James, and Buzz Aldrin. *Space Atlas: Mapping the Universe and Beyond*. London, England: National Geographic, 2011.

Index

A
absolute magnitude 19
absolute zero 66
alien life-forms 24
Almagest 9
Anaximander 8
Andromeda 100, 108
anthropomorphic universe 13
antihydrogen 93
antimatter 93
aperture 16
Apollo Missions I–XVII 129–33
Apollo Program 129
apparent magnitude 19
arcs of fire 39
Arecibo telescope 23
Arend-Roland Comet 47
Ariel 59
Aristotle 8, 10
asteroids 26, 27, 28, 34, 138
astronomers 19
Astronomia Nova 31
atmospheric density 35
atmospheric distortion 19
atoms 41

B
barred spiral galaxies 110
beta particles 96
Bethe, Hans 70
Big Bang 12
Big Crunch 14
binary stars 82
biography of a star 35
black hole 69, 90
bodies in motion 44
Borrelly Comet 46
Braun, Wernher von 118
bright spots 40

C
Callisto 33, 55
carbon dioxide 52
Chandrasekhar, Subrahmanyan 70
Charon 61
chromosphere 40
chronology of space engineering 120–1
Clarke, Arthur C. 138
classical astronomy 8–10
clouds of hydrogen 29
collision, galaxy 112
comet tail 46

comets 27, 34, 46–7
constellations 72–5
convection zone 37
convective layer 37
Copernicus 10
core heat 37
corona 38, 40
coronal loops 40
cosmic debris 42
crescent moon 43
Cygnus 77

D
dark matter 92, 98
daylight comet 47
De Rerum Natura 8
dimensional space 95
distance in space 18
Drake, Frank

E
Eagle Nebula 20, 66
Earth 32, 36–7, 50
earth wobble 23
eclipse 38
Einstein 11, 94
ejecta 44
electromagnetic force 95
electromagnetic spectrum 17
element factories 70
elliptical galaxies 110
energy 37, 41
equator 38
Eris 27, 61
Eros 34
Europa 33, 54
extinction of dinosaurs 34

F
first quarter moon 43
fossil fuels 41

G
Gagarin, Yuri 121, 124
galaxy 100
investigating 100–114
Galileo 10
Ganymede 33, 55
gas giant 29
gases 38
Gemini Project 127
Gemini-Titan IV 126
giant Contact Lens 21
Glenn, John 125

globular cluster 83
God's snowballs 46
Goddard, Robert 118
Grand Unified Theory 94
gravitons 95
gravity 62, 95
Great Wall 107
greenhouse gas 35

H
Halley, Edmond 62
Halley's Comet 47
Harmonices Mundi 31
heat production 37
Heisenberg, Werner 70
heliocentrism 11
helium 29, 41
formation 37
helix nebula 87
hemisphere 74
Hertzsprung-Russell diagram 80
Hipparchus 79
Hoyle, Fred 12
Hubble, Edwin 11
Telescope 21, 100, 110
Huygens, Christiaan 57
hydrogen 29, 41, 53, 68
clouds 29
metallic 29

I
infrared radiation 20
Io 33, 54
IR radiation 40
irregular galaxies 109

J
Jupiter 23, 32, 35, 47, 53, 54
composition of 29

K
Kennedy, J.F. 123
Kepler, Johannes 31
Kirch's Comet 47
Kohoutek Comet 47
Korolyov, Sergei 119

L
large mass star 68
launch sites, location 122
Lemaître, Georges-Henri 12
lenses 16
liquid hydrogen 35
liquid propellant rocket 118

local group galaxies 109
Lucretius 8
lunar eclipse 45

M

Magellanic Cloud 64, 105–8
magnetic energy 38
magnetic regions 40
Mars 32, 52
mechanists 11
medium mass star 68
Mercury 32,36,41,48,128
Mercury Program 129
meteor collisions 34
meteors 27, 34
microwave radiation 13
Milky Way 26, 101–104
Miranda 59
Moon 51
  composition 36
  formation 42
  full 43
  last quarter 43
  mass 36
  size 36
  surface 44
  surface gravity 37
multiple dimension theory13

N

nebula 41, 77, 85
neighboring galaxies 105
Neptune 33, 35, 60
  discovery 29
neutrinos 40
neutron 68
  star 81, 89
Newton 11, 62
Nobel Prize 13
nuclear force 96

O

Oberon 59
objects in motion 30
open cluster 84
optical telescope 16
orbiting bodies 32–33
orbits 30–31, 46
  of Jupiter 34
  of Mars 34
  of the Sun 33
Orion Constellation 71
other universes 13
other worlds 22

P

parent planet 33
partial eclipse 45
particles, energy 40
Penzias, Arno 12–13
photosphere 38
planetary nebula 41
planets 32, 48
Plato 8
Pluto 27, 32, 61
Pole Star 75
positrons 93
pressure core 29
primal atom 12
probes 138
Project Gemini 129
prominence 39
Proxima Centauri 64
Ptolemic astronomy 9
Ptolemy 8, 9,10
Puerto Rico 23
pulsar 89
Pythagoreans 8

Q

quantum mechanics 70
quarks 93
quasar 114
quasi stellar objects 114

R

radiative layer 37
radio emission 40
radio interference 13
ray craters 44
red dwarf 67
red giant 41
refraction of light 16
resolution 11
Revolutionibus Orbium
  Coelestium 31
rocket engines 116
rockets, early 118
Roman Catholic Church 31

S

Sagittarius 101
Salyut space station134
satellites and probes 136–139
Saturn 33, 35, 56, 57
  rings of 29
scale of universe 6
Seki-Lines Comet 47
SETI 24

Seyfert Galaxy 112
Shakespeare 14
Shoemaker-Levy Comet 47
signals in space 24
solar cycle 39
solar eclipse 44–5
solar flares 39
solar limits 29
solar system 26–63
solid fuel rocket 116
Soviet engineering 119
space exploration 116–141
space investigation 16–24
space race 123
space station 133–5
spectra gas 80
spectrum 17
speed of light 39
spiral galaxies 111
Sputnik 120, 138
star 64–5
  brightest 78
  cluster 83
  companions 82–3
  composition 35
  death 87
  investigating 64–89
  life cycle 66–7
  magnitude 78
  surface 37
  wobble 23
star, mass 81
starlight 79
steady state theory 12,13
Sun 40
  biography of 37
  convective layer 37
  core 40
  diameter 37
  energy 40
  mass 37
  radiative layer 37
  temperature 37–8
supernova **68**, 88–9
  remnant 86
surface temperature 28
Swift Tuttle Comet 47

T

temperature 38
Thales 8
thermonuclear fusion 35–7
third law, Kepler 31

time 36
Titan 57
Titania 59
total eclipse 45
trigonometry 18
Tsiolkovsky, Konstantin 118
Tuttle Comet 47

U
ultraviolet radiation 20
umbriel 59
units, space measurement 71
universe
    composition 92
    end of 14

expanding 11
exploration 8–10

matter 92–98
    size of 6–7
Uranus 33, 35
    discovery 29
UV radiation 40

V
V2 118
Venus 32, 35, 41, 49, 89
Viking II 141
visible radiation 40

Vostok 124

W
weight 62
West Comet 47
white dwarf 41, 68
Wilson, Robert 12–13
Wolf Comet 47

Y
yellow dwarf 81

Z
zodiac 76–7

Photo Credits

The publishers would like to thank the following for permission to reproduce images.

NASA: pp 6, 21, 22, 33, 34, 36, 39, 42, 44, 46, 48, 49, 50, 51, 52, 53, 54, 55, 56, 57, 58, 59, 60, 61, 65, 67, 69, 71, 82, 83, 84, 85, 86, 87, 88, 92, 97, 102, 104, 106, 107, 110, 111, 112, 113, 114, 115, 119, 121, 126, 127, 128, 129, 132, 133, 135, 136, 139, 140

Science and Society Picture Library: pp 9, 10, 11, 30, 31, 94, 120

Richard Burgess (illustrator): pp 17 (b), 20, 26, 29, 32, 38, 40, 43, 45, 74, 75, 76, 77, 80, 101